Bible, Bhagavad-Gita
&
Billionaires

Bible, Bhagavad-Gita & Billionaires

Vamsi Palem

PARTRIDGE
A Penguin Random House Company

ISBN: Hardcover   978-1-4828-1949-6
            Softcover   978-1-4828-1948-9
            eBook   978-1-4828-1947-2

To order additional copies of this book, contact
Partridge India
000 800 10062 62
www.partridgepublishing.com/india
orders.india@partridgepublishing.com

TABLE OF CONTENTS

FOREWORD

Dear Readers,

First of all, even before I start, I would like make one thing very clear. I am not an authority on Bible or Bhagavad-Gita, not even by a far means. Many a great men have dedicated their entire lives to decipher the timeless teachings and preachings of Lord Jesus Christ and Lord Krishna. Many a great treatises have already been written on each and every chapter of the above two books. Nope, I am not trying to expound these great teachings to you guys. No, No, No . . . . hundred times a big "NO"!!

Secondly I am not a billionaire. Again, not even by a far means. As a matter of fact I am neither a millionaire nor a lakhier. Like millions of people in this world, I am a monthly salaried guy. I honestly don't know how to make a Billion dollars or Million for that matter.

Then who the hell do you think you are to write a book on Bible, Bhagavad-Gita and more importantly Billionaires? You bet we are interested in that last word.

Of course I bet. As a matter of fact, I am more than 100% sure that it is the word "Billionaires" rather than Bhagavad-Gita or Bible which aroused your curiosity towards this book . . .

Oh C'mon . . . . admit it!!

This simple or rather humble effort is not to give you tips on how to make easy money or how to become a billionaire overnight (there is nothing like overnight Billionaires in this world), but to bring to your notice how some of the billionaires implemented (Knowingly or unknowingly) in their daily lives some of the teachings elucidated in the two great books and why they are where they are, why they are who they are & most importantly why they achieved what they achieved. Just to bring to your notice. Nothing else.

Does spiritual wealth make a man prosperous? I firmly believe it does. Surely it is not a coincidence that India ranks 4th in the number of Billionaires of the world. There must be some reason. At least I am sure.

Many a times when we see some men (Ok women too . . . . Don't want to start a sexist controversy), we wonder what they have in them what we don't and more importantly *what they have done* to deserve what they posses. When we hear about Bill gates or Steve Jobs or Ambani brothers or Laxmi Mittal or Amitabh Bachchan or Tiger woods or an Oprah Winfrey or an Abdul Kalam or Akio Morito or Mother Teresa, of course my all time hero . . . . Swami Vivekananda . . . . we just can't help wondering "Why god why? Why am I one in the million ants that live and die? Or why can't I be some one like that? Why can't I make an indelible mark on this world like them? What have they done to deserve it? Just what have they *done?*"

And mind you, when I use the word Billionaires, I necessarily don't mean Billionaires with Billon dollars in their bank balance. Some have billion fans, some have billion followers and some have billion devotees. Some have a billion admirers. Some one's lifetime achievement is worth more than any Billion dollars. The answer to the above question is in the question itself. They have "**done**" something to get what they got. Doing something, Karma, the action in the right direction in the right time or right way gave them the results. Karma!! Does the word sound familiar? Heard it some where?

And in this humble attempt of mine, I couldn't help noticing that all the billionaires and all the super achievers had many of the qualities mentioned in the two holy books. Hence you will find some of the names getting repeated again and again in most of the chapters. Most of the information I mentioned in this book about the great personalities, I either got it through internet or I have read their autobiographies. As a proud Indian, I have also mentioned the names of some exemplary Indians who I think are already very famous throughout the world. But just in case you haven't heard, I strongly recommend to all the readers around the world to go through their lives and achievements. My dear readers around the world, I am sure you can catch a glimpse of their greatness. Who knows? May be you can absorb some of it.

Now let's get down to the actual reading and see how all the stupendously successful personalities have embedded in them . . . . some where or other . . . . the profound preachings of the timeless books . . . . as a matter of fact, always timely books.

And . . . . all the best.

Acknowledgements

First of all, I would like to thank, of course the almighty for planting the seed in my mind to write this book and giving me strength and will power to persevere to finish the book. I honestly can't tell you how many umpteen number of times I wondered if I am up for the task. As a matter of fact, writing this book puts an extra onus on me to live a life of some really high standards . . . . doesn't it? My sincere prayer to the dear lord once again to be with me and help me to live up to the standards that would be expected out of the author of this book. My advance acknowledgements for the same.

I would like to thank His divine Grace A.C.Bhaktivedanta Swami Prabhupada, founder—Acharya of international Society for Krishna Consciousness for his classic translation of Bhagavad-Gita through his book "Bhagavad-Gita As It Is". This book has not only been my guide at a very personal level, but also the reference for this book.

Next, I would like to thank my mother Mrs. P. Bhagyamma whose inputs and interpretations from Bible have been of invaluable contribution to this book.

I would like to thank my one year old son Dhiren, who is blessed with the loveliest smile in the world . . . . Yes kiddo, you brought a new dimension, meaning and a higher purpose to my life.

Thank you to you my dear wife Sandhya, you constantly encouraged me and brought a sense of urgency to the completion of this project which I undertook.

I would like to thank the developers of MS word with all its wonderful features (which every one takes for granted nowadays) without which I would not have started this book at all. Nope, if I was born 50 years ago and had to write all this with pen and paper, I would not have started it at all.

I would like to take this opportunity to thank the developers of internet whose exact developer I couldn't know, even after I searched in the internet extensively ☺. But who ever you are, thank you sir(s).You played a very big role in the completion of this book.

And I would like to thank you all my dear readers in advance for picking up this book in the hope of improving your lives. I know one thing about you my dear reader. As curious as you might have been when you picked up this book seeing the title "Bible, Bhagavad-Gita and Billionaires", am sure at some corner of your heart, you had some hope to improve yourself. Didn't you? I sincerely hope I won't disappoint you.

God bless all.

John 10:10
I am come that they may have life and they might have it more abundantly.

John 1:2
"Beloved, I wish above all things that thou mayest prosper and be in health, even as thy soul prospereth."

Proverbs 13:8
Poverty and Shame shall be to them that refuseth instruction.

Bhagavad-Gita:Chapter3: verse 21
What ever Action is performed by a great man, common men follow in his footsteps. And whatever standards he sets by his exemplary acts, all the world pursues.

Bhagavad-Gita:Chapter11: verse 12
If hundreds of thousands of suns rose up at once into the sky, they might resemble the effulgence of supreme person in that universal form.

HIGHER SELF CALLING

The word "Self realization", as often interpreted as something monastic or something strictly used in ochre robe circles does not necessarily mean the same. The word Self realization holds equally good among circles where Armani Suits and Bentley cars are flaunted around. Every Billionaire who made it big or "large" answered the call from higher "self" or "god". The rest (Money, fame, fanfare) followed automatically. They just decided to follow their goal given to them by their own higher self. I use the words "higher self" and God interchangeably. As a matter of fact, I prefer to use the word higher self rather than God. As religious as I am, God indeed is a slightly obscure concept, at least for me and am sure for many of us.

And follow the lives of any billionaire carefully. Almost every body before becoming a billionaire could have cocooned themselves in a comfortable life of mediocrity or their reasonable success and decent livelihood.

Legendary Indian actor Amitabh Bachchan could have happily settled in a job in All India Radio. Reigning superstar of the country Shahrukh Khan had a cozy job in MarutiUdyog Ltd. Narayana Murthy, the founder of Infosys, the first Indian company to be listed in Nasdaq could have continued with his job in Patni computers. Bill Gates could have finished his degree in Harvard and settled with a comfortable job. Every Billionaire could have happily settled down well before they became billionaire. But what pushed them or pulled them or nudged them to tread on paths very few mortals dare is nothing but a voice deep down in their hearts or shall I use the word "Higher self"?

Let me give you list of all the people who were quite comfortable or rather big even before they made it large or gigantic.

Arnold Schwarzenegger was already a Mr. Universe and a seven time Mr. Olympia before he became the Hollywood Superstar or rather the Terminator. And what I find even more fascinating is how he went on to become the governor of California (Governator).

Sameer Gehlaut, the business man touted as the next big one in the country had a comfortable job in the Halliburton, US before he came back to India and started the pioneering online trading brokerage firm **India bulls** just 12 years back. Today he is the world's 92nd richest person (as I write this book). Calling his success a meteoric rise would be an understatement.

Rajeev Chandrasekhar, the Telecom tycoon who never got the due he deserves in terms of fame had a dream job in Intel, Silicon Valley.But he comes back to India, starts BPL mobile and today he is speculated to have a wealth worth 1.2Billion $.

Sunil Bharti Mittal, the poster boy of the Indian telecom industry was already worth more than 250 million Rupees with telephone business before he ventured Airtel and today the chairman and group CEO of Bharti enterprises, more commonly called telecom mogul of India has a net worth is 8.3Billion $.

French born Bernard Arnault, the fourth richest person(as I write this book) in the world, owner of the world famous luxury brand Louis Vuitton was well placed comfortably by 1981 in Florida with a net worth of 40 million francs with his construction company Ferinel Inc. which developed condominiums in Florida. But he did not stop there. He came back to France to buy out the Boussac, an ailing Textile group and as they say, the rest is history. Today his wealth weighs 40 Billion $.

Carlos slim, the richest person in the world in the year 2012,was already a millionaire by year 1965 with a net worth of 40 million $.Today through his holdings in the conglomerate Grupo Carso, his worth is 69 Billion $ and more notably he is the richest man on the planet.

Mother Teresa could have lived a comfortable life as sister in an established convent. On 10th September 1946, Teresa experienced what she later described as "the call within the call" while traveling by train to the Loreto convent in Darjeeling from Calcutta for her annual retreat. "I was to leave the convent and help the poor while living among them. It was an order. To fail would have been to break the faith". Mother Teresa felt the call to serve the poor, the destitute, the lepers and the naked (As mentioned in her Biography) and she plunged herself to the service of mankind. Today her "Missionaries of charity" are spread across 123 countries. And the whole world knows what she has manifested.

Jeff Bezos, an Alumnus of the Princeton University, was having a super comfortable life with a well paying job in New York hedge funds. But he started his online merchant company called amazon.com in 1994 in a small garage and today his wealth is estimated to be around 24 billion dollars. From a monthly salaried guy to 24 billion dollars in a span of 18 years . . . . phew!!

Marc Russel Benioff was already a vice president (ya . . . . vice president, a designation many a people have as their life's ambition) in oracle. One fine day he decided that he is not going to work for another billionaire SOB. Today he is one of them. Billionaire that is. He started salesforce.com in an apartment in San Francisco and today his net worth is 2.4 billion dollars.

So what motivated the above people to reach for the stars when they had already reached the moon? I coin a new term here to answer the question . . . . "Call from higher self". It is the call from the higher self which propelled them to the zenith. Keep reading.

Bhagavad-Gita:Chapter 3: verse 21

What ever Action is performed by a great man, common men follow in his footsteps. And whatever standards he sets by his exemplary acts, all the world pursues.

Lord Krishna in the above verse emphatically declares that there is in-deed a great man and in-deed a common man. What separates the two? I hinted in the first sentence itself. Their deeds of course. Let me repeat. What makes one exemplary and what makes one common is nothing but their deeds. It's as simple and as straight forward as that.

Next comes the question; what drives these men to do the great deeds they did?

Answer is . . . .

Their duty!!! Yes their duty. Hmmm . . . . You surely were expecting some very hi-fi word which a GRE topper needs to refer the Webster dictionary to find the meaning of . . . weren't you? Nope, the answer is "Duty". A word which we hear and use in our day to day life umpteen number of times. The only difference is that a common man's duty is assigned to him by the external world and the great man's duty is assigned to him by his own internal world or his own higher self. Observe carefully the life of any self made man. The job they finally landed themselves was appointed to them by their own self. They were self driven or self motivated or self initiated.

Phrases like "self driven" or "self motivated" have become more of clichés in management circles, but calls for a deep introspection and a thorough observation into our own self, our own lives. Are we indeed self driven? Only we know the answer. Yes, only ourselves. And a Billionaire's answer to above question is always "yes". A bold and emphatic "Yes"!! They always answered the innermost call from their OWN higher most self.

And if you ask me how to find in the maze of thoughts and desires that keep roaming in your mind, which one are you going to construe as the call from your higher self, I don't know. I honestly don't know. How I wish God calls us by name and assigns us his plan for our life, as he told Moses or Joseph or David during the Old Testament times or Lord Krishna told Arjuna what his immediate duty is. Phew . . . . how much confusion our good Lord would have saved us?

But unfortunately, our good lord doesn't work that way anymore in 21st century. Why not so? Why so? . . . well, well, well . . . . and the answer is, I don't know again and more importantly, no point arguing with God. But again, I don't think that Good lord met any 21st century billionaire in flesh and blood either and told him what to do. Then how do you conclude what to do? I'll suggest you the answer.

Of all the thoughts, random desires which roam relentlessly in your mind, some thought, some desire, some idea . . . . it just sticks. For e.g., the idea to write this book for yours truly. I just knew it. I have to do it. And here you are, reading this book.

And indeed "An Idea **can can can** change your life". Believe me and more importantly believe **your** idea. As one billionaire very rightly said "For the world to believe in your idea, you must believe it first". After all, if you yourself don't believe in your idea, what chance do you stand in convincing the world about the efficacy of your idea?

The thought may spring up in your mind any time, any where, out of no where. Sometimes when the thought lingers in your mind for a while and it refuses to leave your mind, give that thought a thought. I repeat **give the thought a thought**. Give that Idea a thought. May be that thought is the call from your higher self. Who knows . . . . may be!!

Matthew 6:21

For where your treasure is, there will your heart be also

Are you able to put your heart into your present work? Are you really able to treasure your job or output of your job? If from depth of your heart your answer is yes, then continue. Take pride in your job. Believe that God by placing **you** in **that** job completed this world or a better way to look at it is "God needs you to be in that job for a fulfilled earth". Believe it and make the best out of it.

Let's just take the converse of what Jesus Christ said.

"If your heart is not there, it is just not your treasure". Agree with me? I continue further . . . . assuming so.

Some times, a deep sense of frustration, unhappiness permeates your inner self. You introspect yourself with utmost sincerity, you analyze yourself, you thoroughly scrutinize yourself. But naa . . . . the frustration refuses to go. You take some creative steps to fight your frustration. And naa . . . . again! The fugitive frustration refuses to go.

Probably life is trying to poke you, to tell you something, to teach you something, to point you towards something. I firmly believe in something at a very personal level. A sentence I read in the iconic book "Wings of fire" written by our beloved ex-president & the Rocket man of India, Dr.Abdul Kalam. The sentence goes like this.

"Those which obstruct instruct"

Probably that small piece of unhappiness obstructing your happiness is trying to instruct you something. Probably you are in the wrong job or in the wrong place or probably, time has come to move on to do something else. Probably, it is nudging your heart to look out for something or shall I say look *in* for something. Probably, Probably, and Probably!! All the way I use the word "probably" because I know there is no rock hard mathematical provable way to prove what I say. So I stick to "probably".

George Clooney, the Hollywood hero, in a movie awards function very wisely said "If you are not happy at what you are doing, do it better or do something different". May be the unhappiness is a prod, telling you to raise your bar of your current work or to do something different or to double check where your heart is. Probably! Have a look into the below examples and you will realize it is some form of unhappiness or negativity that brought out the greatness of the individuals.

Steve jobs in his famous speech in Stanford mentions how the tasteless classes in his college lead him to attend his calligraphic classes and we all know he went on to create Apple and more importantly we all know what his Apple created.

VAMSI PALEM

Ratan Tata during his reign as top honcho of the Tata Empire suffered severe loneliness and despondency for the initial 5-6 years which prompted him to take up the break through passenger car project and we all know Tata Indica car is a part of Indian world now. And we all know what he went on to achieve and accomplish. Today Tata Empire is worth more than 83 billion dollars, by far the biggest conglomerate in the India, not to mention the accolades that line up behind the illustrious Ratan Tata.

Narayan Murthy, the chief mentor of Infosys goes on to tell how the deep frustration that accumulated during his tenure in Patni computers, thanks to the hierarchical culture of the Patni computers lead to the genesis of Infosys. And well, Infosys needs no introduction today.

JK Rowling (Joanne Rowling) went through the most traumatizing personal life experiences before she rose to riches and fame; of course thanks to her Harry Potter Series. Well, as per latest grape vine her net wealth is worth 1Billion $.Not a bad going eh . . . . for a divorced unemployed single mother diagnosed with clinical depression just 20 years ago.

Soichiro Honda suffered a devastating bomber attack which ruined his manufacturing plant for piston rings during the Second World War which lead him to dispose of his piston ring plant to Toyota. And with that money as investment he started Honda. And today I don't need to tell anyone about the brand they call "Honda". There is hardly any country in this world where Honda manufacturing plant (Either two wheeler or four wheeler) or dealership is not there.

In the Great Indian Epic Mahabharata, Arjuna had to suffer 14 years of exile before he received the eye opening tutelage(Bhagavad-Gita) from Lord Krishna and went on to win his Kingdom.

And last but not the least; Jesus Christ suffered the most repugnant of the indignities in the hands of Roman soldiers before he resurrected himself. And saying he has a Billion devotees or followers is mother of all understatements. Agree with me?

The list can go on & on & on. But I guess you get the point. Whether the story is historical or mythological, message is . . . . pain alias negativity always, yes, always gives birth to something. Both metaphorically and literally! Dear Reader, your mother suffered severe pain to give you birth. So I go back to one of my previous statements. If there is any residue of pain inside, take a hard look at it and do something about it. The pain may be nudging you to look upwards towards your higher self.

The very fact that you are giving that frustration a thought escalates you into the top 3% of this world population. As a matter of fact, many a men continue to live "happily" in this world with that unhappiness. Many a men accept this frustration as a part and parcel of life and more importantly they convince themselves that that's how life is supposed to be. I personally conducted a small survey in shopping malls, railway stations, bus-stands. I asked one question to every body "Are you 100 % happy?". Almost everybody said "No". Some people went to the extent of saying that "no body can be 100 % happy." Oh yeah? Really? As I already said common man always believes that certain unhappiness or some form of negativity (frustration, anger, despair, sadness, and unfulfilled desires) is part and parcel of normal life. But a billionaire always does something about the lurking negativity. As a matter of fact, Author of self help classic "Awaken the Giant within", Tony Robbins goes on to say "Success comes out of always doing something about negativity" in his one of the all time best sellers.

Call from the higher self always lurks inconspicuously behind the negativity. Just peep around the unhappiness and the call can be the one which can lead you to happiness, riches, fame & prosperity. And all the billionaires answered the call. They backed themselves to the hilt to follow that call and success followed . . . . inevitably.

Just see what Lord Krishna Says below I would recommend all my readers to read the following three versus again and again and again till the essence of them gets dissolved into each and every droplet of their blood and nerve cells.

Bhagavad-Gita Chapter 3: verse 21

It's a lot better to perform one's prescribed duties even though in faulty manner, than doing other's duty. Wrong happening in the course of performing one's own duty is much better than engaging in another's duties, for to follow another's path is worse.

Bhagavad-Gita Chapter 18: verse 47

It is better in one's own occupation even though one may perform imperfectly than to accept another's occupation and perform it perfectly. Prescribed duties as per your core nature are never smeared by sinful reactions.

Bhagavad-Gita Chapter 18 : Verse 48

Faults or mistakes are part of every effort, just as smoke is a part and parcel of every fire. Hence one must not give up the work which is born out of his own nature, O Son of Kunti, even some faults roll out in the process of doing such work.

My dear Readers, read the above three verses from lord Krishna again and again and again . . . . can the Lord ask you more succinctly to follow your heart? Can he encourage you more? Can he more openly say "It is ok to do some mistakes"? Can he more openly ask you to introspect yourself and find your own nature? And more importantly, can he shout louder to do something which resonates with your own core nature? Read the above three verses again and then the below verse from New Testament.

Romans 12:4-12:7

For as we have many members in one body, and all members have not the same office;

So we, being many are one body in Christ and every one members of another

Having then gifts differing according to the grace that is given to us, whether prophecy, let is prophesy according to the proportion of faith;

Or ministry, let us wait on ministering; or he that teacheth, on teaching.

Can St. Paul tell you more crystal clearly that just as each part of body has a very distinctive purpose, each and every one of us in this world has a clear cut out purpose? Can St. Paul explain better that each and every one has been bestowed with a separate gift and our works should be according to our gifts? During St. Paul times, am sure there weren't as many professions as today. So he stuck to ministry and teaching. But today, that's not the case. There are innumerable opportunities and innumerable professions and of course world has become more accepting. Art, Music, painting, cooking, haircutting (there are millionaire hair stylists indeed !), stand up comedians, singing, story telling . . . take any field you want and there are billionaires who made it to the top and who have become rich and famous. All of them have committed themselves to the duty their higher self has allocated to them. Definitely not by anyone else . . . . nope . . . definitely not.

My dear readers, do the above verses from Bhagavad-Gita and Bible penetrate your heart and mind? Are you really doing your duty given by your own higher self or are you doing the duty given to you by some one else? Is your work or job really complementing the "gift" given to you. Ask yourself. I can't emphasize the importance of serious contemplation of the above subject which I coined as "higher self calling" and more importantly abiding by the call. An hour or day of serious honest introspection can be life changing. And why not go for it? The Lord himself has given us the lenience to do some mistakes in the path. He even goes to the extent of saying, doing mistakes in the path of *your* duty is better than doing your non-duty perfectly.

Following your heart, doing something that resonates with your nature always brings peace of mind, sense of satisfaction and more importantly sense of accomplishment. Ask any billionaire and he must have done something which truly represents his nature, his deep innermost core nature and the best of him came out naturally and money, fame, success followed as a natural by product. I re-iterate something which I already mentioned previously more than a couple of times. Common man's "duty" in all probability is externally appointed and billionaire's "duty" is always internally appointed by his own *very own* higher self. Yes . . . . always, always, always

A small story from Old Testament which I find appropriate at this juncture . . . .

Almost any Christian would have read the story of Jonah in Old Testament. He was given a certain straight forward instruction by God to go to the city of Ninevah. But what does he do? He goes exactly in the opposite direction to some other city. And what happens? He gets thrown overboard the ship; gets gobbled by a fish and is finally puked out. After he is puked out, what does God ask him to do. The good lord asks him to go to the City of Ninevah . . . . the same instruction Lord gave at the beginning. Good lord did not change his instruction by a single letter. And Jonah had no choice but to abide by the command.

Now my dear Readers, please allow me to tweak the above story a bit to contemporary times. Are you constantly being thrown overboard, gobbled or puked out or puked at(literally or metaphorically)? Then my dear readers, perhaps you are travelling in the wrong direction. Perhaps it is time to re-evaluate yourself. Perhaps time to look deep with in your self and your hearts or perhaps pray to heavenly father to show the right direction. Ask the creator to let you know what the true purpose of your life is. Why are you planted on this earth. And . . . .

Mathew 7:7

"Ask and it shall be given; Seek, and ye shall find; Knock and it shall be opened unto you"

. . . . you will receive your call from higher self. If your prayer is sincere and yearning is honest, you will receive the answer, the call. That call will surely resonate with your nature . . . . core nature . . . true deepest core nature. It will be the direction given by and to your true self.

The call will definitely help you to "know thyself". Lest it appears that I am not giving this topic called "know thyself" its due, let me tell you "knowing thyself" is much much much beyond the scope of this book. The one who already knows thyself need not read this book at all.

In his acclaimed book, "21 secrets of self made millionaires", by Brian Tracy, Tracy clearly tells one simple fact. All the billionaires love their work. That's because it just resonates with their core nature. They do it out of love. Not as a drudgery. I realized that discussing these religious topics in the light of contemporary times comes naturally to me. I could spend hours discussing importance of spirituality in modern times. There were days I came home after a very busy day in office. But once I start writing this book, things kind of flowed automatically and as a matter of fact, I felt refreshed *after* writing a page or couple for this book for a time period of hour or two. It didn't take long for me to realize that this work indeed is very much in accord with my core liking. And yes, this is true for anyone on this earth.

Let me explain you better. Am sure many of you can relate to what I am going to tell. You observe in your own office . . . . assuming your office timings are 9am to 5pm . . . . who gets promoted faster? A guy who can comfortably work till 7 pm or a guy who through adamant determination works till 6 pm or a guy who keeps looking at his watch from 4 pm eagerly waiting for the "times up" bell and rushes home punctually at 5 pm? No prizes for guessing. Mind you, am not ridiculing or berating the last guy. Nope, not at all. Perhaps the work just isn't his inner taste. Nothing wrong with that at all. But the problem is not many "last guys" introspect themselves and find out what they are meant for. They blame it on fate or destiny or whatever. And they conveniently assume the guy who zoomed ahead in their lives and careers are lucky. They never even ask themselves "What do I really like?"

And as a result, they do injustice to both their job and employer. Perhaps you can get away with it. But shall I tell you the blunder you just cannot get away with? You are doing injustice to yourself. And trust me guys . . . . that is one hell of a gigantic blunder you are never ever going to get away with.

Well, you may scoff of at me . . . . Don't I know what I like? Well my dear readers, then tell me something. If everyone knows what they like, why are there so many unhappy people around the world. Because, not everyone introspects. Well, the word introspection is just more than a word, it's a concept. A concept with unfathomable importance. A thorough impartial dissection, scrutiny, analysis and more importantly judgment of our own self. No wonder people spend half their lives understanding their own self. And no wonder "Know Thyself" has been given such a prima donna status in the Christian philosophy.

Steve Jobs in his famous speech at Stanford very rightly said, you have to find what you love and the love affair with your job gets better and better with time. Your work life occupies major portion of your life. And what Steve Jobs said is true for every billionaire. All the billionaires just loved their jobs or the fields they excelled in. They loved their jobs with their heart and soul and from every single nerve cell of the three trillion nerve cells in their body. It appears to be common sense. Just see the below examples.

Can you imagine Arnold Schwarzenegger going to gym as a duty and working out as a routine job?

Can you imagine Michael Jackson practicing his steps as an office work or "lets get it over with" attitude?

Can you imagine Michael Jordan training (his training sessions are stuff of legends) with a grim face because his coach asked him to?

Can you imagine Bill Gates tinkering with computer in his early days because his class teacher asked him to?

Can you imagine Ustad Zakir Hussain playing tableau peeking at his watch and waiting eagerly for the end of the practice session?

Can you imagine Walt Disney drawing his animations because someone put a gun to his head?

Can you imagine APJ Abdul Kalam or a Von Braun with no love for warfare rocketry?

Can you imagine Brain Tracy or Zig Zagler the world renowned public speakers with no natural talent for public speaking?

Can you imagine a Sidney Sheldon or Jeffrey Archer or a Michel Crichton writing their novels as a part time job or just to supplement their income?

Just observe in Hollywood. Some of the all time biggest block buster movies are director's or producers' pet projects.

They loved the projects from their inner most hearts. They **wanted** those projects to materialize. And the grandeur and the magnificence of the outcome movie (Of course the commercial Success) was a natural by product. Benhur by William Wyler, Jurassic Park by Steven Spielberg, Terminator 2, The Judgment Day by James Cameroon, Lagaan (Hindi Movie) by Aamir Khan were outcome of love and passion for the movies by the respective directors.

Can you imagine any CEO or managing director who does not love what he does? As a matter of fact, no one would rise so high in an organization unless he likes what he does at a very personal level.

Enough of "Can you imagine"!

(Talking about the word love, any grown up adult knows you cannot intellectually fall in love with something or someone. You cannot tell yourself . . . . "ok this is my job, so I have to fall in love with this". Nope it doesn't just work that way. Love is something connected to heart not brain. First you fall in love with your heart and then you intellectually decide that this is my love and go for it whole "heart"edly. Agree with me? . . . . hope so my dear readers.)

A classic example I would like to quote here . . .

Uday Kotak, the founder of **Kotak Mahindra**, tells how right from his childhood he had a fascination for numbers and it was his inclination to choose a career involving lots and lots of numbers which initiated him into the financial sector. Today(as I write this book), Kotak Mahindra is India's third largest private sector bank. Today his market cap is 67000 million Rupees. A classic example of how a natural childhood talent blooms into a gigantic success!

The list can go on and on and on . . . . But my dear readers, I hope all of you are seeing the point I am trying to make clearly. All the people and personalities I mentioned in the above examples used their ***natural gifts*** to their fullest.

See what the good Lord Jesus Christ has to say in the New Testament.

John4:34

> My meat is to do the will of him that sent me and to finish his work.

Are we really doing the will of the one who sent us down here to the earth? Are we really enroute finishing the work assigned to us? How many of us can say "yes" from bottom of our hearts? Am sure not many of us can. But a billionaire can say "Yes". "Yes" it is . . . . always.

Mathew 7:21

> "Not every one that saith unto him, Lord, Lord, shall enter into the kingdom of heaven; but he that doeth the will of my father which is in the heaven"

Did Jesus Christ compliment what he already said in John 4:34? In Simple terms, you do the will of god and you will reach the heaven. Period. All the billionaires did the will of god which I coined "call from higher self". All of them did reach the heaven while still alive ☺.

I summarize the above chapter in to following 5 steps.

1. Ask yourself if you are 100 % happy with yourself and your life?
2. If not, ask your self why not?

3. Thoroughly introspect yourself and ask yourself what will make you 100 % happy?

4. When you get the answer, construe it as a call from your higher self and go for it. Don't be afraid of mistakes. The god lord himself said that mistakes are very much allowed. Just learn from mistakes and just keep going.

5. Billions (fans, followers, admirers and of course money) follow automatically.

I conclude this chapter with the following verse from the Redeemer.

Mathew 5:16

Let your light so shine before men, that they may see your good works and glorify your father which is in heaven.

Is your light shining bright enough for the world to see and is able to glorify the creator for creating you? Ask yourself. I'll not elaborate further. I believe I had elaborated enough already. As I already said . . . . "INTROSPECT" . . . thoroughly and shine on . . . . brightly.

FAITH, BELIEF, SELF CONFIDENCE

Call it whatever you want

O k . . . . you finally decide what you are meant for . . . . You zero in on "God's will" for you . . . . your call from your higher self. What happens next? Doubts start arising from your mind.

Am I up for the task?

Am I capable to do it?

What If I fail?

What if I cannot do this?

What will the world say?

Am I out of my mind to let go a well beaten path and try something risky or weird?

Am I nuts to let go a secure job and try my hand into something risky which may end me up on the streets?

What If I let down my family?

These are indeed genuine questions. These are very much the practical doubts. Nothing cynical or pessimistic about them. I'll come to answers of the above questions in the later part of this chapter.

But before I go further, answer a small question . . . .

How many times does Lord Jesus Christ use the word Faith in his preaching?

How many times does Lord Jesus Christ use the word Belief in his preaching?

I did not count, but the reason why Jesus Christ used those two words again and again and again and again is, if any one quality that needs to be drilled deep into our head, if any two words needs to be stapled right onto our hearts, it is faith & It is belief. Faith in ourselves, Faith in God. Belief in our selves, Belief in God. Take any self improvement book, any motivational lecture from any motivational speaker, any preaching from any prophet, they put paramount importance on self belief, faith in self. As a matter of fact, in many a books I studied, the very first chapter is "Believe in yourself".

Mark 9:23

"If thou canst believe, all the things are possible to him that believeth"

Mathew 9:29

"According to your faith be it unto you"

Mathew 17:20

"If ye have faith as a grain of mustard seed, ye shall say unto this mountain, remove hence to yonder place ;and it shall remove and. nothing shall be impossible to you"

Mathew 15:28

"O Woman, great is thy faith: be unto thee even as thou wilt. And her daughter was made whole that very hour"

Mathew 21:21

"If ye have faith and doubt not, ye shall not only do this which is done to the fig tree, but ye shall say unto this mountain, be thou removed, and be cast into the sea; it shall be done"

Mathew 21:22

"All things what so ever you ask in prayer, believing, ye shall receive"

Mark 5:34

"Daughter, thy faith hath made thee whole ;go in peace"

Mark 5:36

"Be not afraid, only believe"

Luke 17:6

"If ye had faith as a grain of mustard seed, ye might say unto this sycamine tree, be thou plucked up the root and thou planted unto sea and it should obey you"

Luke 18:42
"Receive thy sight, thy faith hath saved thee"

The sayings go on and on and on . . . . Read the above sayings again and again till you get a feel of the importance of "faith & Belief".

Now a saying from 20th century's Dr.Maxwell Maltz, the legendary author of the Psycho-Cybernetics . . .

> "With in you right now is the power to do things.The power comes to you just as soon as you change your beliefs"

From Henry Ford . . . .

> "Whether you believe you can do it or whether you believe you cannot do it . . . . either way you are right"

From Emerson . . . .

> "They conquer who believe they can".

Mind you all the three gentlemen are superlatively successful. Do their achievements walk their talks? Of course they do.

Again I ask you, why did Jesus repeat and repeat and repeat words "Belief, faith"? Ask yourself. Pause for a while . . . . think over it carefully. Try to get an answer yourself. Because absolute belief, absolute faith is an absolute pre-requisite for achieving some thing, anything for that matter. Dispelling your doubts and a firm belief in yourself is a must to walk the extra mile to achieve something big. For a long time I too thought that "Faith can move mountains" is a biblical rhetoric. But as I observe more and more successful people, as I study the lives of more "billionaires", the above saying appears to be mere common sense. Yes . . . . nothing but mere common sense.

Firm belief & faith that you can do some thing opens up the paths to your goal. Psychiatrists have more than umpteen number of times re-iterated that positive thinking is one of the most important quality of any successful human being. Positive thinking is no-Rocket science. It just a belief that something good is coming to you or you are going to get something good come what may. It's just a firm belief that there is something good in everything, every situation, every circumstance, every difficulty if you look for it. If you believe that you will eventually reach your goal, every situation that comes in the way will be nothing but a stepping stone and a pointer in the right direction that you are going in the right way. See the below saying from Thomas Alva Edison. "I did not fail 1000 times . . . . but I discovered 1000 ways it won't work". World knows what Edison went on to manifest in his lifetime.

Self belief gives you courage to start.

Self belief gives you the energy to work.

Self belief gives you the perseverance to keep moving.

Self belief gives you the strength to convince others the efficacy of your idea.

The most fantastic example I can give of self belief is Sir Roger Bannister. Rather, how Sir Roger Bannister was taken as an example by several athletes to boost their self belief. Almost any sports enthusiast knows about Roger Bannister. But in case, if anyone doesn't know about him, here I go.

Sir Roger Bannister (Roger Bannister was knight hooded in 1975) was the first athlete in history of mankind who ran a mile under 4 minutes. For several years, from pre-olympic times, it was "believed" by all humans that if a human tries to run a mile under 4 minutes human heart will explode. Only God knows how that belief came into existence. But it did come and the "belief" got embedded into human hearts and brains & what happens? Nobody true to the belief ran a mile distance under 4 minutes till 6th May 1954, the day that belief was broken by Roger Bannister. "Well . . . . Nothing fascinating about it" you may say. May be. But what fascinated the mankind in those days is the fact that in the same year nine more athletes ran the mile barrier under 4 minutes.

So what changed? Did the human anatomy change? Nope, of course not. The only one thing which changed is human belief. The Knight has been or rather *is* credited to have changed the human belief. And who knows, it may be the same belief in himself that made Sir Roger Bannister to go on to become one of the most distinguished neurologists of his time.

Think about it again . . . . would any billionaire take the first step if he didn't have the belief and faith that he is going to make it big?

Would Narayan Murthy start Infosys, if he did not "know" before hand that some day his company is going to make it big?

Would Sylvester Stallone keep trying again and again despite being rejected by more than 1000 agents before he became the action star? Some where deep within his heart he must have believed or he knew that he was meant to become what he went on to become.

Would Bill Gates drop of college to start of his Microsoft without some belief deep rooted in his heart that Microsoft is going to become Big?

Would Martin Luther King.Jr start the Civil rights movement if he did not have belief in the fulfillment of his "dream"?

Would Mahatma Gandhi start his non violence movement against the British Empire if he did not believe in the eventual victory of his approach?

Would Shahrukh Khan leave a comfortable job in Maruti Udyog(the manufacturers of Maruti Cars,the most sold cars in India) and come to Bombay without a mustard seed of faith in himself that he's going to make it big?

Would Amitabh Bachchan leave a comfortable job in All India Radio and come to Bombay without any faith in his dream of becoming an actor?

Would Chatrapathi Sivaji take the might of the Aurangazeb's Moghul Empire without an iota of faith that he is going to succeed?

Would Arnold Schwarzenegger come all the way to America from Austria without faith that he is going to be the next biggie in the world of body building ?I can't think of any migrant in America who lived a more voracious American Dream. From a champion body builder to Movie star to Politician. He is one hell of "Done it all . . . . seen it all" guy.

Would Jim Carrey write himself a Cheque of 10 million dollars in 1987 dated 1995 for the "acting services rendered" with out some belief in his heart about his comic capability? (He went to demand 20 million dollars per movie by 1995. His comic block busters Mask, Ace Ventura minted money to say the least).

Would David Packard and William Hewlett have taken their company Hewlett Packard public in 1957 with out any firm belief in the capability of their brain child to make it big?

Would Colonel Sanders have kept trying to sell his franchise for his secret recipe of fried chicken despite being rejected for 1008 times without a firm faith in the efficacy of his recipe?

Would yours truly start writing this book without faith in himself? I don't mean to brag, but hope all my dear readers agree that some where deep inside my heart, I trusted I am up for the task. And here you are reading this book.

The list can go on and on and on. Go through the above list once again. It will not take a genius to figure out that at some corner of their hearts, they very well new that they are going to succeed well before hand. And more over if you look at the above mentioned examples, just see the odds they were up against (scratch my own example). All the billionaires knew what they were up against. But in every case their belief got the better of the odds. And the reason is simple. They just believed they were going to get what they desired eventually. And they did.

John 4:4

"Ye are of god, little children, and have overcome them: because greater is he that is in you, than he is that is in the world"

Read the above verse once again. Can the Good lord encourage you more?

Why was an entire chapter in Bhagavad Gita devoted to topic called faith? Lord Krishna in the entire chapter clearly explains how a man is what he is only due to his faith. His beliefs.Whatever he is . . . . Ignorant or wise or demonic . . . . What ever he is, it's due to his sheer faith and his sheer beliefs. He clearly says that it is our beliefs and faiths that make us what we are.

In Bhagavad Gita, Lord Krishna for innumerable number of times called Arjuna some great names "o great warrior" "O Scion of Bharata" "O mighty one" . . . . what for??

For one simple reason . . . . he wanted to restore belief and faith to Arjuna in Arjuna himself. All the lord wanted to do was to shake of the despondency and remind Arjuna who he was . . . . "An ace warrior". At least I can't think of any other reason.

As I said earlier, "Self belief is an absolute pre-requisite" is not some biblical rhetoric. It's more of common sense.

I would like to share a small personal experience with you. You may not have exactly the same experience. But am sure you can relate to something similar from your own life if you introspect. Here I go.

I first learnt car driving from a certain driving school way back in 2008.But, for some ridiculous reason, I always thought it has to be some kind of supermen dropped from sky to be capable of driving a car in the actual traffic and for four years (Ya . . . . four years!!), I could not muster enough courage to buy my own car. At last in 2012, I bought a car and once I bought my own car and started driving, I realized that driving a car is no big deal (No offence to anyone who takes pride in driving).All it takes to drive a car is a human being with a pair of hands and pair of legs with an alert eye. I wasted four years of my life without enjoying a car drive. And suddenly a bigger lesson dawned on to me.

"Perhaps I am not doing many other things because I believe I can't, not because I can't. Perhaps this is the same case with many people around the world. May be they are not trying to go after their dreams only because they believe they cannot, not because they are incapable"

One more example from my own humble life . . . .

A particular subject I thought (believed) was difficult during my college days remained difficult for almost 8 years of my professional life just because I believed so. Whenever, during my professional career, I faced any problem involving the subject, I somehow evaded or "cleverly" handed it over to some other colleague. One day, don't know what sparked it, but something sparked an adamant determination in me to understand that subject. And can you guess how long it took to understand that subject? Four hours . . . . just four tiny hours. And I for almost a decade avoided that subject due to some nonsense belief inside me that it takes an Albert Einstein or Isaac Newton to understand that particular subject. The subject that I am referring to is "Turbo charger mapping to a diesel engine". Any Internal combustion engine engineer would know the topic.

I quoted the above two examples just to tell you, how some times or rather most of the times it is our own baseless beliefs which define our acts and boundaries of acts.

Think about it my dear readers . . . . think about it. All it takes to achieve anything for that matter is a human being with belief that he is capable of achieving . . . . that's it . . . . full stop . . . . period. All it takes to achieve anything is a human being with a pair of hands and legs with an alert eye (both literal and metaphorical) who believes that he can achieve.

I bet you would have read this before. "Most of the barriers of human being are self imposed. As a matter of fact, most of the barriers are barriers only because we believe they are barriers". I couldn't agree more. See the picture coming up. It's a picture one of my friends in Facebook shared. Indeed as funny as it is, I can't help realizing the magnitude of the message it holds for the entire mankind.

The horse for some god forsaken reason believes that it is tied up and it is immobile. The one kilo plastic chair is refraining the horse to move!! Silly . . . . isn't it? The horse can run away with the chair effortlessly if it tries to. But it doesn't . . . . why? Just because the horse firmly "knows" that the chair is immovable.

Another classic example is an elephant tied up to a small stack of grass or some metal rod wedged into ground to a depth of 6 inches. Saying an adult elephant can yank away the wedge out of the ground effortlessly is an understatement. But it doesn't. Not because it cannot, because it believes that it cannot. I assume all of you know how an elephant is trained to believe that it cannot rip out the wedge from ground.

My dear readers . . . . are you getting the point . . . . Are you clearly seeing what I am trying to say? Do the above examples corroborate the fact that "most of the barriers are barriers only because we believe they are barriers"? Now only god knows how many things we are not doing because we "know" we cannot.

Vivek Paul Ex-CEO of Wipro Technologies, after seeing a tied elephant in a circus realized that most of the boundaries are indeed self imposed. He encouraged all the Wipro employees to bust their limits on the boundaries. And a result . . . . he ramped up the revenues of Wipro from $150 million in 1999 to $1.4 Billion by 2004.Almost 10 times growth in a span of 5 years! One can only fathom the self belief Vivek Paul must have had.

And I am telling you this from my own experience. Most of the people don't go ahead chasing their dreams because of self doubts. Self doubts may appear to be genuine. You may back your self doubts with references from your past. Perhaps you did not do too well in your school. Perhaps in the initial phase of your career you did not get the same appreciation or hikes your peers got. Perhaps you could not take a female of your dreams out. But all said and done, doubt is nothing but a thought that springs in your mind. Past failure is nothing but a bitter memory or a good lesson if you are willing to learn from it. No need to put more importance to that. Just let it go and go ahead with your **Call from Higher Self.**

Tony Blair in his autobiography "A Journey" clearly mentions how he was plagued by his own self doubts during the early phase of his political career. What really mattered was he refused to succumb to his self doubts. Every one has self doubts the Ex-British prime minster insists. Self doubts are nothing but some ridiculous thoughts that spring from your mind. "Don't doubt yourself because you have self doubts". A line to be noted from the Ex-British prime minster's Auto Biography. And when the gentlemen who ruled Great Britain for 10 long years says something, there must be more than an iota of truth in his words and I take those words to letter with out any further arguments.

Again I re-iterate, many a times, with many a people that's the case. People just don't try anything new not because they are incapable, only because they believe they are incapable. May be the barriers or the road blocks are not as big as they seem to. May be the terrain to your goal is not as rough as it appears to be. May be you are not as weak as you think you are. There definitely are going to be hurdles in this life or journey called "chasing your dreams". But all it takes my friend is a "mustard seed of faith to cast out the mountain of hurdles into the sea". And nope, this is not a biblical rhetoric.

There are plenty of examples in the history of mankind and the examples are growing in number in the modern times about successful people who have defied the common beliefs and cemented their places in the annals of mankind.

Look below and see some of the examples of common beliefs (misbeliefs) and the examples which (who) mock at those beliefs.

"*I wish I had a more imposing personality to become a leader*" . . . . oh yeah??

Mahatma Gandhi with his 5'3" frame shook the roots of the British Empire.

Adolph Hitler with a height of 5'8" wreaked havoc in the world as no one else ever did.

Stalin with his height of 5'4" led the Russians to a spectacular win in the Second World War.

"*I wish I had a degree from a good business school to make it big in business or I wish I was born in a family with a huge ancestral property to have huge wealth*"

The above myth has already diminished by several degrees thanks to umpteen number of dot com billionaires who sprouted out of the Silicon Valley over the last 2 decades. Silicon Valley is dotted with number of dotcom billionaires who started virtually with nothing and went on to become millionaires or billionaires. Yes, most of the dotcom billionaires are not MBA grads. But nevertheless, I'll tell you some of my all-time favorite real life stories.

Dhirubhai Ambani was barely a graduate. He went on to establish "Reliance" a business empire of 12 billion dollars during his life time.

Shiv Nadar, founder of HCL, a 4 billion$ software enterprise was an electronics engineer (No MBA) who did not even see a city till he was 22 years old.

Narayan Murthy and his 6 partners(none of them MBA) started of Infosys with a investment of 10,000 rupees and today his wealth keeps fluctuating between 1.4 billion and 1.5 Billion $.

I honestly don't know if they started with exact figures in their minds . . . . but one thing I am 100 % sure is they were 100 % sure that they were going to make it big if not today . . . tomorrow . . . . if not tomorrow . . . . the next day . . . . but sure they were. Allow me to re-phrase. They were 100% sure they had to make it big.

I recommend all of you to read the book "Connect the dots" written by Rashmi Banal. There are some amazing stories of people with not so impressive back grounds, not with some hi-fi degrees, who just followed their inclination and how they made it big. The above mentioned book has certainly been one of the catalysts that triggered my self belief to write this book.

"I wish I had a better physique for chasing my career in acting."

Aamir khan, the most celebrated actor in Indian cinema is 5'5".

Tom cruise, one of the highly paid Hollywood actors is 5'7".

Akkineni Nageswara Roa, the legendary Telugu (My Mother tongue) actor was a numero uno of Telugu movies for over 30 years. You know what his height is . . . . 5'5".

Somewhere they believed in their other abilities to make up for their deficiencies.

They had to . . . . there was no other choice if they had to make their dreams come true.

Now you may ask . . . . referring to the first questions I mentioned in this chapter about all the common doubts that hurdle our taking the first leap of faith. Well there is no standard operating procedure. And I don't know how any billionaire discarded his or her self doubts when he or she started. I am not even sure whether they discarded the self doubts or not. It's highly probable that they did not discard at all. But one thing am sure is that they went ahead despite the self doubts.

"Don't doubt yourself because you have self doubts"-Tony Blair

How they suppressed their self doubts, I know not. But what I am sure is that they consciously faced their doubts. They consciously faced their fears. They weren't afraid of failure and they firmly believed that their perseverance can outlast the duration of failure. But a couple of sentences in Bible and Bhagavad-Gita that have always boosted not only my self confidence but that of millions of people around the world . . . . I have recited the below sentences again and again to myself whenever I felt low.

Philippians 4:13
"I can do all things through Christ who strengeneth me"

Luke 17:21
"Kingdom of god is with in you"

Romans 8:31
"If god be for us, who can be against us"

John 4:4
"Ye are of god, little children, and have overcome them: because greater is he that is in you, than he is that is in the world"

Bhagavad-Gita Chapter 18: verse 61
"The supreme lord is situated in everyone's heart, O Arjuna, and is directing the wanderings of all living entities, who are seated as on a machine, made of material energy"

See the innumerable numerous ways god tries to encourage us. If the above quotes cannot encourage you, I don't know what else can.

Read the above sayings from the holy books and tweak them for your convenience if you want. "Kingdom of god is in me . . . . god is with me and nothing can be against me . . . God is in my heart and he will guide me in the right direction".You can repeat them day and night till the above sentences' meaning is tingling in your every drop of blood. You can give your self a pep talk standing in front of mirror or while driving your car. Anyway you like. But do it till the belief becomes embedded into your nook and corner. But do believe in yourself. Every Billionaire did. Every billionaire firmly believed that some divine energy is situated in their hearts and what is **in** them is greater than what is **outside**.

Some billionaires in the god out side them . . . . Some billionaires in the god inside themselves. Some or other form of belief they clinged onto. But believe they did. And today their names are etched in the history as firmly as carved on stone.

WORK, WORK, WORK

After you get a call from higher self, which you are most welcome to construe as a call from god, what do you do? You ramp up your self belief. You pep up yourself to believe that you can achieve. What next? Well, another simple answer . . . . you act . . . . you work. You put some efforts in the right direction.

If there is any one word in Bhagavad-Gita which Lord Krishna repeatedly and repeatedly and repeatedly shouted his lungs out . . . . its "Work" "Work" and "Work". As a matter of fact, two chapters of Bhagavad-Gita (Ch.3 and Ch.5) are dedicated exclusively for sake of this word called "**Work**". Lord Krishna puts so much emphasis on **"Work"** that he goes on to say that a dedicated worker is better than any ascetic or a swami or any god man and working with dedication is faster way to reach god (the Supreme) than renouncing loved ones and meditating atop Himalayas or in some ashram as the common notion goes. Read the below verse.

Bhagavad-Gita Ch5: verse 2

The blessed lord said: The renunciation of work and work in devotion are both good for liberation. But, of the two, work in devotional service is better than renunciation of works.

Can the blessed lord be more succinct about the importance of work? Can he be?

The phrase "work in devotional service" has a lot of religious connotation in a common man's perspective. The word "devotion" inevitably brings to our mind a devotee in temple with closed eyes & folded hands or someone in church kneeling down with clasped palms. Indeed praying with devotion is a very important aspect of our life. For me too, it is of paramount importance. But Lord Krishna, in the above verse makes it very clear that devotional work outside the temple is as important as praying inside the temple to attain the supreme.

Are we able to approach our day to day work with a devotional attitude? Whether you are a software engineer or a lawyer or a teacher or a doctor or any professional for that matter . . . . are you able to answer the call anointed to you by your own higher self with utmost devotion? Introspect yourself. If the answer is **yes**, then it is well and good. All is well indeed. You are indeed on your way to becoming a billionaire. Trust me.But if your answer is "no", then you better start to devote yourself to your duty (the duty I mentioned in the Chapter no.1) right away.

Bhagavad-Gita Chapter 5: verse 5

One who knows that position reached by means of renunciation can also be attained by works in devotional service and who therefore sees that the path of works and the path of renunciation are one, sees things as they are.

The above phrase from lord Krishna re-iterates the importance of working in devotion. In our professional circles we use the word "commitment" instead of devotion.

And you don't need to be a Sherlock Holmes to observe a simple fact. The top brass of your company are extremely committed individuals. The elite rich and famous of this world, the "who and who" of this world are by default workaholics. You can take this fact for granted. They are sheer workaholics. The word work-aholic may be detested by some as it sounds like some pathological negative condition. But it certainly conveys the meaning. Even the greatest of the greatest Indian saints and philosophers Swami Vivekananda and Swami Paramahansa Yogananda lead an immensely active and a productive life. Yes, extremely active and productive.

Swami Vivekananda (Swamiji as he was lovingly revered) in his famous speech "practical Vedanta" clearly mentions how the greatest of the philosophers and teachers were monarchs or Kshatriyas. He goes on to explain why it is such. At this juncture I recommend all of you to read the treatises and speeches of Swamiji. And I have no problem in admitting that Swamiji can elucidate the importance of work far better than me. One sentence I quote from Swamiji's acclaimed lecture he gave in London.

"The doctrine which stands out luminously in every page of the Gita is intense activity, but in the midst of it, eternal calmness". Greatest of the knowledge and rewards descend upon the busiest and the most engaged human beings the Swamiji concludes.

Have you ever observed one simple fact in Bible? Abraham, David, Solomon, Job, Joseph (Old Testament) . . . . all the characters as much as faith they had in God were extremely wealthy in their contemporary times, some of them were kings with huge earthly responsibilities. In modern times they would have been termed as very busy guys. **Wealth indeed descends on to busy guys**. A simple fact which the above mentioned gentlemen amply demonstrated!

Even two of the most followed deities in Hindu religion Lord Rama and Lord Krishna were Monarchs. Lord Krishna imparted his highest knowledge to one more **Kshatriya,** a prince from King's dynasty, the Arjuna. Getting the point?

I from my own humble experience know for sure that a deep sense of satisfaction, a feeling of pride and silent elation descends upon you on the days you have been very productive rather than on the days you have killed your time in the office despite the mental exhaustion. The hike in your self esteem is immeasurable. I am 100% sure that every professional knows what I am talking about. Even the most incompetent of the incompetent employee knows what I am talking about.

James 2:14-2:26

What doth it profit, my brethren,though a man may say he hath faith, and have not works? Can faith save him?

If a brother or sister be naked, and destitute of daily food

And if one of you say unto them, depart in peace, be ye warmed and filled;not withstanding ye give them not those things which are needful to the body what doth it profit?

Even so faith, if hath not works,is dead being alone.

Yea,a man say thou hast faith,and I have works;shew me thy faith with out thy works,and I shall shew thee my faith by my works

Thou believest that there is one god;thou doest well;the devils also believe and tremble

But wilt thou know,O vain man,that faith without works is dead?

Was not Abraham our father justified by works,when he had offered Isaac his son upon the altar?

See thou how faith wrought with his works,and by works was faith made perfect ?

And the scripture was fulfilled which saith,Abraham believed god, and it was imputed unto him for his righteousness:and he was called the friend of god.

Ye see then how that by works a man is justified, and not by faith only.

Likewise also was not rehab the harlot justified by works, when she had received the messengers, when she had received the messengers, and sent them out another way?

For as the body without spirit is dead, so faith without works is dead also.

Read the above verses again and again until you are sure that you have grasped the fullest meaning of it. Please read it several times.

All the above verses were spoken by James, a direct disciple of Lord Jesus. James as much as he knew the importance of belief & faith(He was a direct disciple of Jesus Christ. Who could have known better?) goes on to say again and again, unless you do, unless you act, unless you implement, unless you work, all your faith and staunch belief in yourself and God is a sheer waste. Common sense isn't it? I personally believe in something. Faith and Work make a closed loop. They form the alternate links of the chain which you hold on to climb up your lives and reach your goals. Faith initiates work. Work reinforces faith. Both have to be backed up by both. Lack of either can prove to be the fatal link in your failure. As a matter of fact, my personal interpretation from the above preaching is "Lord sees or rather checks if we are backing our so called faith and belief with commensurate magnitude of work or if our belief has become an excuse for laziness & lethargy and if we are avoiding what **we are supposed to do**". Putting forth tangible work to materialize our faith in the direction of our goal is a **must on our part**. As a matter of fact, our working towards our goal shows that we are positive. It shows that we believe in the materialization of our dreams and goals. Think for a while. Its common sense again.

Again I re-iterate what James Said

James 2:26
For as the body without spirit is dead, so faith without works is dead also.

Take a page out of the lives of the below mentioned billionaires armed of course with their supreme confidence and self belief and see for yourself the magnitude of spirited work, spirited action, spirited effort that they put forth . . . . Oh yah . . . . it takes hell of a spirit to put forth the magnitude of work they did.

Arnold Schwarzenegger in his body building Classic "Encyclopedia of body building" mentions how he worked out 5-6 hours a day in gym (I know personally what it takes to exercise 5-6 hours a day at a stretch) and the results speak for themselves. Knowing that, his going on to win Mr. Universe at the age of 20 and Mr. Olympia a record seven times need not surprise anyone. In one of his famous speeches he plainly says the most important rule to success is "Work your butt off" and believe in yourself. And the champion body builder, Movie star and the politician tells the one of the foremost lesson he learnt in his life is "There are no shortcuts . . . . You have to earn it". And to earn something you need to work it out. Today I have not seen a single gym or fitness equipment selling shop without a poster of Arnold Schwarzenegger.

Jeff Bezos's first rule to success is "Act". It is only through deliberate action that we can bend the universe to our will. Action bends the universe to our will? Unfathomable for ordinary mortals . . . . isn't it? But when a guy with 24 billion dollars (24,000,000,000$) in his pocket says something there must some truth in it. Further words of wisdom from the Alumnus of Princeton and also the founder of Amazon. com, the world's largest online merchant store; "If you decide that you're going to do only the things you know are going to work, you're going to leave a lot of opportunity on the table". **After all, doing mistakes teaches you more than doing the right things. So keep doing something.**

Dr. Abdul Kalam, the Rocket man of India speaks of his 80 working hours a week during his days in DRDO (Defense Research Development Organization) and its definitely not an exaggeration to say that, if India today is force to reckon in the field of war rocketry in the eyes of the world, its due to the supreme efforts of the above mentioned great man. And of course, Abdul Kalam getting conferred with the Bharat Rathna, the highest civilian award for an Indian need not surprise any one again.

Will Smith, one of the most respected actors says as candidly as anyone else "while the other guy is sleeping, I am working. While the other guy is eating I am working. Hard work is the key to success. It's that simple." Will Smith's work while other guys are sleeping and eating has made him one of the most successful movie stars of all times. And of course one of the highest paid.

Narayan Murthy, the founder of Infosys reminisces how he used to work for 16 hours a day during the budding days of Infosys and his being crowned by international accolades and awards(the list of accolades and awards is massive and more over, one more prestigious than the another) seem to be natural cause and effect.

Have a look at the Iconic kungfu legend Bruce lee's daily regime. Lee trained from 7 am to 9 am, including stomach, flexibility, and running, and from 11 am to 12 pm he would weight train and cycle. A typical exercise for Lee would be to run a distance of two to six miles in 15 to 45 minutes, in which he would vary speed in 3-5 minute intervals. Lee would ride the equivalent of 10 miles (about 16 kilometres) in 45 minutes on a stationary bike. Lee would sometimes exercise with the jump rope and put in 800 jumps after cycling. Lee would also do exercises to toughen the skin on his fists, including thrusting his hands into buckets of harsh rocks and gravel. He would do over 500 repetitions of this on a given day. And you know and I know the generations of fanfare athletes and body builders he inspired and continues to inspire in the ages to come.

The list goes on and on and on like the energized bunny. Hardly any Billionaire in this world who doesn't work hard.

As a matter or fact, god or infinite or universe assigned the biggest of the works (Responsibilities) to the biggest of the believers. And biggest of the believers were the biggest of the workers. Moses . . . . David . . . . and of course Jesus himself. Read the biblical stories of the above heroes in new light and you will be able to fathom the magnitude of responsibility put on their shoulders. All of them not only worked, they completed the work assigned to them.

Let me tell you a small parable which Jesus Christ preached. Any Christian knows the parable.

Matthew 25:14

For the kingdom of heaven is like a man travelling in to a far country, who called his own servants and delivered unto them his goods. And unto one he gave five talents,to another two and to another one;to every man unto his several ability ;and straight way took his journey. Then he that had received the five talents went and traded with the same and made them other five talents. And like wise he that had received two,he has also gained other two. But he had received one went and digged in the earth and hid his lord's money.

After a long time the lord of those servants cometh and reckoneth with them.And so that he received five talents came and brought other five talents saying lord thou deliveredst unto me five talents;behold,I have gained beside them five talents more. His lord said unto him,well done thou good and faithful servant: thou hast been faithful over several things,I 'll make thee ruler over many things;enter thou in to joy of thy lord.He also that had recieveth two talents came and said lord,thoudeliveredst unto me two talents;behold,I have gained two other talents beside them.His lord said unto them,well done good and faithful servant,thou hast been faithful over few things,I 'll make you ruler over many things,enter thou into the joy of thy lord.Then he which had received the one talent came and said,lord,I knew thee that thou art an hard man,reaping where thou hast not sown,and not gathering where thou hast not strawed.And I was afraid and went and hid thy talents in the earth;lo,there thou hast that has thine.

His lord answered and said unto him thou wicked and slothful servant, thou knewest that I reap where I sowed not,and gather where I have not strawed:Thou oughtest therefore to have put money to the exchangers and then at my coming I should have received mine own with usury. Take therefore the the talent from him and give it unto him that has ten talents.

Despite the biblical language the moral of the story is very much self explanatory. The more you deliver, *the more*

WILL be delivered to you. The more you are responsible, the more the responsibilities given to you.

As per my interpretation, there is one very important trait Jesus brings to our notice through the above parable.

It is "taking initiative"—Doing something with out anyone asking you to do. Being productive without any one telling you to be. Doing something new. Improving upon something that already exists through self motivation.

Swami Yogananda Paramahansa in one of his famous lectures "power of initiative" goes on to say "If you have not taken initiative to create anything new or done something on your own, you have insulted the unique image of god inside you".

Look into the life of any great Inventor, great entrepreneur, great politician, great leader or any great sportsman. They themselves took the initiative to do what they want to do, what they had to achieve. One of the meanings of word initiative is **"Spirit to originate action."**

The word I want to highlight is "originate". "Origin"ate . . . Heard the word "Origin" some where? Am sure you did. Yeah, the same (0, 0) . . . X coordinate is Zero and Y coordinate is Zero. Understanding what I am getting to? All the billionaires had an origin and they themselves took the action in the direction of their goal. From the origin of their idea, to the accomplishment of their goals they were self driven and self motivated. From the origin to their end goal, the equation of the path was self created. No body asked them to do what they did like the first two servants in the above parable. As a matter of fact I am sure you understand the word initiative better rather than the above rhetoric explanation. Let's talk of the trait Initiative and some of the greatest personalities of the mankind.

Mahatma Gandhi, Father of the Indian nation initiated a freedom movement through non violence, a unique style, the world has never seen or heard about. And the Kingdom in which the sun never set had to retreat before the might of the Old man who had nothing but a walking stick in his hand.

Tony Blair, arguably one of the greatest prime ministers of England wouldn't have been a prime minister in the first place but for the initiatives he took to modernize the Labor party. It was his initiative to look beyond the loyalty of conventional labor unions that firmly rooted him to the prime minister position firmly for 10 years (Of course I cannot write 600 + pages of Tony Blair's Autobiography "A Journey" in a single paragraph).

Thomas Alva Edison as great as an inventor he was, it was his initiative to commercialize his inventions and his initiative to manufacture his Inventions on large scale basis that made him the legend he is today and of course a very very very rich guy in his contemporary times. It was his initiative to spread electricity to the house hold which made his life (Of course all our lives) such a glittering success. Imagine life without electricity!!

As mentioned earlier, it was Mother Teresa's initiative to serve the poor, the needy, the lepers that lead to the establishment of the Missionary of Charity. Her initiative to establish Nirmal Shishu Bhavan, her initiative to establish the Kalighat (Home for dying), her initiative to . . . . her initiative to . . . . her initiative to . . . . the list goes on &on & on. Today no charity organization is established with out somewhere or somehow role modeling Mother Teresa or at least a poster of Mother Teresa in the premises of the organization.

Steven Covey the celebrated author of the widely acclaimed Book "Seven habits of the highly successful people" mentions in his book, the foremost habit of any successful person is his capability to take the initiative, to be in charge of your life, to be pro-active.

It was Swami Yogananda Paramhansa's initiative to spread the timeless teachings of Hinduism that made the word "Yoga" so popular in the west. It was his initiative over a span of thirty years that lead to the establishment of "Self Realization fellow ship Centre", an organized way to spread the teachings and wisdom of the ancient seers. Swami Yogananda's Autobiography "Autobiography of yogi" is by far the most revealing account into the life of a Hindu yogi and Swami Yogananda has been credited to take the initiative for explaining Hinduism with the scientific clarity none has been able to do so far.

Martin Luther King.Jr took the initiative to start a movement for the abolition of the apartheid, racism and slavery of blacks. None should have any problem admitting that indeed King's "Dream" has come true today. His prolific participation in civil rights movement and sanctioning the commonly called the Fair Housing Act shortly after his assassination says it all. The fact that a Black man (Barack Obama) is leading the United States of America today (as I write this book) sums it all. Even today King's Iconic status as human rights activist remains un-paralleled.

Jackie Chan took the initiative to improvise comedy, house hold articles as fighting props in to his fight scenes and more importantly to add stunt goof ups during the shooting of the film at the end of the movie & his popularity as an actor is there to be seen. As popular as he is for those dare devil stunts, his initiative to provide education to the underprivileged makes him one of the most beloved actors of Hollywood.

Dr.Verghese Kurian, widely known as the "Milk man of India" took the initiative to implement the operation flood, the project to grow the annual output of milk in India. From a milk deficient country, India became the world's largest producer of milk thanks to the efforts of the Padma Vibhushan (The third highest civilian award in India) rewardee Dr.Kurian. His initiative to start the movements like AMUL has not only rewarded him, but also millions of dairy farmers their daily livelihood.

Jeff Bezos took the initiative to take full advantage of the budding E-Commerce (budding is an understatement . . . . it was an internet gold rush growing at the rate 2400 % per anum) in 1994 and founded Amazon.com, an online merchant store. Today his wealth is estimated to be around 24billion dollars. Who knows how much his wealth is going to be in another 10 years once his company "Blue origin" starts to get operational. His initiative to "send anybody into space" is as amazing as the Amazon itself. Got to wait and see. He indeed means one of his rules "never stop innovating".

Marc Russel Benioff, the founder of the salesforce.com took the initiative to revamp the way software programs are designed and distributed. He initiated "Platform as service" by allowing customers to build their applications on the salesforce.com cloud. Today he is worth 2.4 Billion dollars. The international accolades received by salesforce.com say it all. Today Salesforce.com ranks as one of the most innovative companies founded in the 21st century.

Walt Disney revolutionized the entertainment industry and Hollywood was never the same again. His creation of arguably the greatest cartoon character ever "Mickey Mouse" has made him one of the foremost millionaires of Hollywood. Today he is an international icon despite half a century after he passed away. It was his initiative to build the world's biggest theme park that made the Disney land a dream vacation spot for almost everyone in the world. Almost any theme park built in the world some where or other copies the Disney land. As a matter of fact, many of the theme parks, water parks are nothing but subset of Disney land.

Soichiro Honda took the initiative to create a two wheeler which consumes the minimum of fuel. He created the "SuperCub". A bicycle with a motor fitted, as some of the contemporaries described or shall I say ridiculed? Irrespective of what others said, It was a matter of time before Honda bike's sales overtook those of Triumph and Harley Davidson (yes,the same bike Arnold Schwarzenegger rode in the James Cameroon's block buster Terminator 2), the two iconic American bikes in America. Yes, IN America.

Jesus Christ took the initiative to spread the Word of god, power of god and more importantly, the importance of the life,how life should be lived and the path of redemption. And . . . . I don't need to say any further.

In case any of my readers are thinking that I have given too many examples, allow me to explain why. I added this concept called initiative in this chapter because hard work & effort as rewarding as they are, will give you success to a certain level. But taking initiative to do something new, to improve on something already present is an absolute pre-requisite to a resounding success. Indeed, it is absolutely unarguable fact that initiating something new takes double the hard work, but definitely infinitely more rewarding. Just look around the modern day business world. It is always the breakthrough, cutting edge, innovative companies which initiated something new that made it large.

See some of the below examples.

Google; Search Engine
Microsoft; Software for Personal Computers
Apple; I pod
Sony-Walkman
Starbucks-Selling coffee in posh coffee shop!
KFC-Selling Chicken Burgers
SalesForce-Cloud Computing
Have I said enough about the power of Initiative? Hope so.

I would like to explain you an another very important facet of hard work.

Proverbs 16:3

Commit thy works unto lord and thy thoughts are established.

The above proverb extols again the importance of hard work in a different way. The more you work the more orderly your thoughts get established and the more orderly your thoughts are the better you work. It's a cycle.one precedes other. Or shall I say one follows the other. (Ok which came first? The chicken or the egg?) Hard work gives rise to correct thoughts and correct thoughts give rise to superlative work. I can vouch for the above statement. I myself, many times got the correct idea *after* I plunged into work. Even for writing this book, many a times the right thought came to me after I sat in front of my laptop, not while I was watching TV or not when I was whiling away my time on some meaningless things. Contrary to the common opinion that, great ideas give rise to great works, many times the fact is great works give rise to the great ideas and of course great ideas give rise to greater works.

Swami Paramahansa Yogananda in his famous speech "Answered Prayers" clearly mentions "the more we use our will power and put practical effort the more the divine will help us. You don't need to coax. Divine in his own accord wants to help us". Or simply put, God only helps those who help themselves. The more you help yourselves the more you will be helped by the right thoughts that sprout out.

Thomas Alva Edison summed it all far better than any one else.

"Genius is 99% perspiration and 1 % inspiration". Observe carefully the above saying. Which came first? Perspiring hard work or an Inspiring thought? Did Edison make a point which parallels the above proverb (**Proverbs 16:3**) from Bible? Certainly . . . . I think so and hope my readers agree.

In my mother tongue language, Telugu, there is a saying which I'll translate for all of you.

"Mountain sized effort may be there, but nail bit of luck is needed". See the converse of the statement. Before one expects nail bit of luck, mountain sized effort is needed.

James Watt got the Idea of a centrifugal Governor during his prolific research on steam engine. And the industrial universe was never the same again. Its not an exaggeration to say that fulcrum of the industrial revolution was the centrifugal governor invented by James Watt. An article I read about James Watt goes on to say "World was never the same again after James Watt's Invention of the centrifugal governor".

Alexander Fleming's "accidental" discovery of Penicillin was perhaps an accident in the most of the eyes of the world. But let me remind you, Alexander Fleming already had a reputation of being a great researcher and his discovery came out of extensive research on staphylococci and more importantly out of a very noble thought to find an effective antibiotic which can cure the wounded soldiers in the war.

Who can disprove that lord established Fleming's thoughts to discover what he discovered? May be it was providence's reward for all the hard work he put forth till then.

Arnold Schwarzenegger recounts in his Autobiography "Total recall; My unbelievably true story" how during his rigorous regime, he got some ideas which made his work out more effective. In his all time classic "Encyclopedia of Modern body building" he clearly mentions how he intuitively came to know how he can trick his own mind to do the reps he planned to do despite excruciating physical pain.

Christopher Columbus discovered United States of America when he was *trying* to find a sea route to India from England. Can anyone disagree that divine altered his mental compass to show the route to America?

I cannot prove . . . . but one thing is certain the more committed the above mentioned gentlemen were towards their work, towards their goal, the more established their thoughts became in the right(required) direction. And it is my strong conviction that providence rewarded them with some pleasant surprises and rewards in the form of the correct strategies for their untiring efforts.

Bhagavad-Gita Chapter 9: verse 22

"To men who meditate on me as their very own
ever united to me by incessant worship, I supply
their deficiencies and make permanent gains"

In the above verse Lord Krishna makes it clear that he will supply the deficiencies and give permanent gains to devotees who incessantly worship him. By incessant worship, Lord Krishna means incessant efforts. Understand it very clearly. Put incessant efforts in the right direction and necessary things will be given. May be the right thought, the right idea . . . . may be you will be guided to the right book, right opportunity. May be you will be connected to the right person in Facebook or in linkedin. Whatever is needed for the fulfillment of your duty or goal shall be given to you, one way or other. Even if you are having some deficit in some areas, it shall be debited to you one way or another. But incessant worship, incessant commitment to your duty, incessant tangible efforts towards the fulfillment of goal given to you by your higher self (god) is an absolute pre-requisite from your side. As I mentioned earlier, I know from my humble experience of writing this book that many a times the right thought came to me after I sat in front of my laptop to write this book, not while watching TV or while I was chit chatting with my friends. There were times when I was searching in internet for information about one personality and I was directed towards other great personalities whom I have mentioned in this book.

Does the above observation of mine second what Martin Luther King. Jr said just half a century ago? "Take the first step, rest of the stair case will be shown". But taking the first step, putting the first effort in some or other direction is definitely your responsibility . . . . yah definitely your responsibility.

As a matter of fact, if you look into Bhagavad-Gita, what was lord Krishna saying to Arjuna all the way in his eighteen chapters?

"You fight . . . . I lead"

"You fight . . . . I guide"

"You fight . . . . I protect"

"You fight" is common and inevitable. You have to fight your own fight. The more you fight (Work), the more you get protected, the more you fight (work) the more you get guided, the more you fight (Work) the more you get leaded.

Even the converse of the above sentences is true.

"No fight . . . . no one to lead . . . . no fight . . . no one to protect . . . . no fight . . . no one to guide"

Read any religious book or self improvement book and see the paramount importance that is emphasized on human effort. Brian Tracy in his best selling book "Eat that Frog" tells if you act boldly, unknown forces will come to your rescue and guide you more towards your goal.

So I re-iterate in one sentence what I was saying above.

"The more you fight (Work), the more you get protected, the more you fight(work) the more you get guided, the more you fight(Work) the more you get leaded"

Yes, I can vouch for that. So again . . . . Keep WORKING

And let me tell you one more facet of hard work and deliverance or rather non hard work and non deliverance to be precise. Please observe the below quote by Lord Jesus Christ.

John 15:2

"Every branch that beareth not fruit he taketh away and every branch that beareth fruit, he purgeth that it may bring forth more fruit"

As a matter of fact, the above quote by Jesus Christ very much goes hand in hand with the Mathew 25:14 parable. First servant and the second servant in the parable were made rulers over several things because they bore fruits, so that they could bear even more fruits and the third servant was cast (removed) away because he did not bear any fruit at all in the first place. Hope my dear readers agree with my analogy.

The more responsibilities you carry out, the more responsibilities will be entrusted to you. Look at any CEO, top honcho's of any multi national company (MNC) . . . . would they have been entrusted with such high responsibilities, had they not delivered when smaller responsibilities were given to them? Ask yourselves and it doesn't take an Albert Einstein to know the answer. The answer is of course "No". It is sheer common sense. Then why do so many struggle hanging in middle of the corporate ladder with out reaching the pinnacle? I know not for sure. Perhaps as Mark Twain remarked "Common sense is not all that common". See the below examples and see for your self that more you bear the right fruits, the more you will be pruned.

Lord Arthur Wellesley, more commonly known as the Duke of wellington is a classic example. Hailed as one of the finest military commanders of the British Army, his military record is exemplary. His first major assignment was in India, where he led British to decisive victories against two of the strongest forces against British at that time, Tipu Sultan and the Marathas. Needless to be surprised, he was later entrusted with the war against France in the peninsular war, where he established himself as the conquering hero and of course he was entrusted with the battle of waterloo where he cemented himself in the history forever by capturing Napoleon. His appointment as the chief commander of the British army and his remaining there for over a quarter century till his death says it all about the consistent delivery of the duke of wellington through out his career. He was the branch who produced more fruits and naturally he was more and more pruned.

Ratan Tata, the retired chairman of the Tata sons, who cemented himself as one of the greatest business tycoons ever in the history of India started of his career in Tata steel by shoveling coal in to steel furnaces. How did he reach the top? Why was he hand picked by JRD Tata, the then charismatic chairman of the Tata group? And more importantly why/how did he remain at the top for over two decades? The answer is because Ratan Tata delivered both before reaching the top and more importantly after reaching the top (*My dear reader . . . . in case you are scoffing of at the obvious answer, ask yourself, how many times did the above "easy answer" cross your mind in case you ever introspected yourself or in case you observed any leader who reached the top by starting at the bottom. Are you really "delivering" the responsibility that has been given to you? If from depths of your conscience your answer is yes, you can be equally sure of one more thing, higher responsibilities are going to be entrusted onto you in no time. You can be sure of that*). In 1971 Ratan Tata was appointed the Director of NELCO, National radio and electronic's division. In 1981 he was appointed the chairman of the Tata Industries Ltd and in 1991 he was elevated to Chairman of the entire Tata Group. In 2007,Business Magazine "Fortune" announced him as one of the most 25 powerful and dynamic businessmen in the world. Does the above anecdote more than sufficiently prove that Ratan Tata was one hell of a branch which bore some superlatively heavy fruits and hence he was more and more pruned for bearing bigger and bigger and bigger fruits and he did bear consistently? Simply put, he converted a 10 billion dollar domestic group into a 100 billion dollar international conglomerate whose tentacles are spread over 83 countries and that too in a span of 20 years. What a dynamic personality!!

Abdul Kalam, the beloved Rocket man of India in his auto biography "Wings of fire" explains the hardships and turmoils he endured and put forth during his early days of his career, the steady responsibilities he carried out in his early days of DRDO till he was picked up by Vikram Sarabhai(Father of Indian space research) to join the Indian Committee for space research and how at each and every step of his ascendency he delivered and surpassed the expectations (of course in his own humble manner).One fine day, he was entrusted with the responsibility of the entire Indian Rocketry. Another fine day he was conferred with Bharat Rathna, the highest award for any civilian in India.

One more classic example is Jack welch, the retired Chairman of GE. During his tenure as the chairman of GE, the group turnover increased by over 4000%.His walk away "gift" was rumored to be around 720 million dollars. He indeed converted 5 talents into 10 talents. He indeed bore more, bigger and tastier fruits he was expected to bear.

So work hard and deliver!

Another very important aspect of the incessant hard work is, it enhances your self belief and self confidence. Hard work enhances your "I can" attitude. A whole chapter I have devoted for the word self belief . . . the previous chapter. Words like hard work, practice, doing, implementation, preparation belong to the same fraternity. But you need to choose the right word depending on what you are. If you are a student you must prepare well . . . . if you are sports person or a musician you must practice . . . . if you are a professional you must implement. After all, the only way to the Carnegie hall is "Practice".

Would a LSAT or GMAT topper approach the exam with an "I can" frame of mind without thorough preparation? The answer is of course not. "I can" frame of mind comes only, yes **only** after some meticulous planning, thorough preparation, sincerely evaluating himself and correcting himself and sincerely writing practice tests. Needless to say, all the above needs some effort . . . . period . . . . no further arguments.

Would a Roger Federer or a Pete Sampras or a Babe Ruth or a Tiger woods or an Ivan lendl enter a tournament without thorough preparation?

"If I don't practice the way I should, then I won't play the way that I know I can"-Ivan Lendl. Ivan lendl played the way he knew he can because he practiced the way he should. His being the only player in the open era whose winning percentage is more than 90% for five years says it all. Pete Sampras in his autobiography "Champion's Mind" narrates how he saw Lendl chalking out his entire coming week's preparation before the start of the week and more importantly implementing it.

Would Dr.Abdul Kalam be successful in launching the "Agni" the first intercontinental ballistic missile without 5 years of rigorous scheduling and implementing in multiple work centers.

So dear readers, ask yourself which category of work, you need to do and **keep doing it.**

Your hard Work or incessant efforts acknowledges one more very very important fact of life. That **time is limited** and you are making the best out of the time available to you. You are making the best use of the most precious commodity or resource that life has given you . . . . "time". Yes, Yes, Yes . . . . time is limited. One fine day it will be curtains down for you. One fine day it is going to be "the end" of your life. Excuse me if am being too dramatic. But it's a fact.

John 9:4

"I must work the works of him that sent me, while it is day: the night cometh, When no man can work"

Time management is no brand new concept indeed. Many modern day speakers have written some very eye opening treatises about Time management. But well, Jesus knew way 2000 years back that time is precious and he must deliver what he needs to deliver in the given time. He iterates metaphorically that one MUST work out the works given to him when it is still a day. Even in our daily lives, for every compartment of life, time allocated is limited. Time allocated for your student phase is limited. Time allocated for your professional phase is limited. Time allocated for your family life is limited, every project and goal has a limited time, a clear cut dead line.

For sake of writing this book, I conducted a survey among the common men and women . . . . people I met in shopping malls, railway stations,bus stations . . . . just ordinary people like you and me. When I asked them what their biggest regret in life is . . . . almost 60% of guys in their twenties replied "I must have studied harder during college" . . . . almost 55 % of people in thirties said "I must have made the best of the opportunities that came my way in my professional life" . . . . and 63% of the people in their fifties and twilight of their life said they regret not taking any calculated risks in their life. They regret not starting something on their own. One old man in his sixties said that even today he regrets not asking his senior colleague to change his department thirty years ago and he was stuck in a department in which he did not have any interest for almost 22 years of his career. But one harsh fact is none of the regret ever changes the past. No amount of regret will turn around the clock back. Well, not at least till somebody invents the time machine.

So my dear readers, time is of essence. And your working incessantly acknowledges the fact; one of the most important facts of life that time is limited and more importantly time is unestimatably precious. You value your time, time values you.

Tony Blair in his Autobiography "Journey" makes a candid point "Show me one bad leader and by default he is a bad time manager. Good leaders must be a good time managers."

Tony Blair hit upon the nail fair and square . . . . didn't he?

2 Thessalonians 2:5

For yourself know how ye ought to follow us; for we behaved ourselves not disorderly among you ;

Neither did we eat any man's bread for nought; but wrought with labour and travail night and day, that we might not be chargeable to any of you:

Not because we have not power, but to make ourselves an example unto you to follow us

For even when we are with you, this we commanded you, that if any would not work, neither should he eat

The speaker of the above verses is none other than St. Paul, a direct disciple of Jesus Christ. If you don't work, you don't deserve to eat. He puts it as bluntly as anyone can.

Bhagavad Gita: Ch 5 Verse 6

The sages purified by works of devotion, achieve the supreme without delay.

And one can work with utmost devotion only if they believe that the work they are doing is going to fulfill the purpose given to them by their higher self(Refer 1ˢᵗ chapter). Lord Krishna clearly says in the above verse "the more work, the more you get purified and more urgently you are going to reach the supreme." Incessant work elevates you to the supreme (Literal and metaphorical) quickly.

So my dear readers, again & again "You got to Work buddy!!" . . . . No other go ☹.

Times of Adversity and A Calm Mind

O k . . . . you begin to work your butts off. Ok . . . . you start getting some good results. Ok . . . . You start gaining confidence, you start getting some positive results, you feel you are on the right track . . . . and then it happens. Yikes . . . . how much I hate to say it . . . . But I have to . . . . ***Life gets in the way***.

You are an entrepreneur . . . . you come to know that your trusted accountant has siphoned out some company funds or misappropriated, embezzled some of your company's money.

You are a student . . . . Just before the final exams, you fall sick.

You are a sportsman . . . . right before a very important match, your calf muscles cramp and refuse to loosen up. All the weeks of tiresome training goes down the drain.

You are a politician . . . . after 15 years of loyalty, party high command does not give you the coveted post you were so eagerly expecting for.

You invest 5 years of time & feelings into a relationship . . . your partner one fine day says that he/she wants to move on . . . . no apologies, no explanations (you are lucky if you get either of them).

Or who knows . . . . the most common complaint of all . . . . you try and try and try for fulfillment of a certain goal . . . . but nothing just happens.

Well, am sure, every one (yes . . . . every one, mind you am not saying *almost everyone*) in this world has/had a taste of some or other form of disappointment, hurt feelings, pain, frustration, despair, anger, hatred, injustice, pangs of excruciating depression, helplessness, despondency. At some or other juncture of their life! Well what you need at that time is . . . . "A calm steady mind". Keep reading.

Bhagavad-Gita Ch.2:Verse 14

O son of kunti, the non permanent appearance of happiness and distress, and their disappearance in due course, are like appearance and dis-appearance of winter and summer seasons. They arise from sense perceptions, O Scion of Bharata, and one must learn to tolerate them without being disturbed.

Bhagavad-Gita Ch.2:Verse 15

O best among men (Arjuna), the person who is not disturbed by happiness and distress and is steady in both is certainly eligible for liberation.

Bhagavad-Gita Ch.2:Verse56

One who is not disturbed inspite of three fold miseries, who is not elated when there is happiness, and who is free from attachment, fear and anger, is called sage of steady mind.

In the above statements, Lord Krishna emphatically declares happiness and sadness exist. They exist as inevitably and as surely as summer and winter. And more importantly, what the lord says is, it is the even minded guy, calm minded guy, who is not disturbed by the vicissitudes of life who is eligible for success. He couldn't be more correct.

"Let not barks of puppies disturb your mind . . . . no, not even the lightning thunders"-Swami Vivekananda. Why did Swamiji (As Swami Vivekananda was always referred as) say the above? Why is it so damn important to stay calm and steady? Answer is simple and obvious (Of course, implementation of the answer is not so easy).

Even mindedness in times of adversity is an absolute pre-requisite to success. Or shall I go to the extent of saying adversity itself is a pre-requisite to success? Take any billionaire, any epitome of success, any celebrity for example. They must have gone through some of the most testing and trying circumstances, a mountain of hurdles and an ocean of problems before they *arrived.*

Every day *must* be preceded by a night.

Every uphill *must be* preceded by a down hill.

Every shore *must be* surrounded by an ocean.

Lest, my dear reader, you think I am talking bookish rhetoric, let me give you anecdotes of men and women in flesh and blood who went through a gamut of troubles before they succeeded. And allow me to make an interesting note here. All the men and women went through the tough times *after* they decided to obey the call from the higher self and some times after they reached the goal given to them by higher self. In case, dear reader, you thought the moment you chase your dreams, life is going to be rosy, you couldn't be more wrong. The real test of character, perseverance, will power comes *after* you decide to abide by the call from your higher self. Nope . . . . not when you have blanketed yourself in some safe & routine job. And even tougher tests come after they arrive at their goal. Yes, Yes, YES,YES . . . . After. And all the way what stayed with them was their rock steady mind. It is a rock steady calm mind, which kept them in their good stead.

As Joe Brandi, the first coach of Pete Sampras told Sampras *after* he won the first US open in 1990 "Now the real work starts".

Now to the anecdotes . . . .

Narayan Murthy, founder of Infosys went through almost 9 incredibly tough years before the company made it big. As a matter of fact, an American company even offered to buy out the company in 1991 when the company's financial condition was in dire straits. But Narayan Murthy clinged on to his convictions and refused to sellout and saying today, Infosys made it big is an understatement. It's the first Indian company to be listed on NASDAQ. And trust me, today many youngsters in India set Narayan Murthy's photo as their desktop for inspiration. Yours truly is one such guy.

Jackie Chan struggled to get a foothold in Hollywood for five years in vain!! Yes, THE Jackie Chan for five years!!Am not sure how many people know that Jackie Chan struggled from 1981 to 1985 in Hollywood before he returned to Hong Kong and became a legend all over Asia. He tried a second comeback in to Hollywood in 1996 with "Rumble in the Bronx" and this time he became a cult figure even in Hollywood and world over.

Bruce Lee the kungfu legend, whose name shall remain till the word "martial arts" exists and whose legendary fitness will be talked about till sun and moon exist suffered a crippling back injury and was hospitalized in an immovable state for months. And shall I tell you something more fascinating? He wrote his book "Jeet kune do" a treatise on art of fighting, while he was hospitalized. Talk of even mindedness!! Not to mention, he bounced back with those awesome movies with those mind boggling fights he displayed in Big Boss, Fist of fury and of course Enter the Dragon! Who can forget the fight with Ohaara (played by Bob wall), the main villain's Bodyguard?

Sylvester Stallone was rejected by more than 1000 agents before he got his first big break in Hollywood. Rocky Balboa's famous speech to his son in the Movie Rocky Balboa may well be the story of Sylvester Stallone's life. Encourage all of you to go to youtube.com and see the famous clip in which he encourages his son to "get what he wants". I must have watched that clip in youtube.com hundreds of times.

Steve Jobs was fired from his own Company (Can we imagine something more humiliating?).Today the late Steve Jobs name is synonymous to innovation and cutting edge. In his famous speech at Stanford's convocation, Steve said "Life sometimes hits you on your head with a brick. But have faith and keep moving".

Tony Blair was in the opposition party for almost a decade and faced a series of defeats before he came to power.

Arnold Schwarzenegger's first rule of success is "Be prepared for failures".

A quote from Andre Agassi's Autobiography "open" I see fit to be written here . . ."Life will throw everything but the kitchens sink in your path, and then will throw the kitchen sink. It's your job to avoid the obstacles. If you let them stop you or distract you, you are not doing your job and failing to do your job will cause regrets that paralyze you more than a bad back(Agassi was suffering from a chronic back pain at the time)." And going through the Autobiography, I must admit that Agassi's life was no bed of roses as one would have imagined. He went through his share of turbulent times and abysmal lows.

Take the example of King David . . . . Ya . . . . the same guy who got Giant Goliath with nothing but a sling in his hand(Old Testament).Life indeed threw every thing but the kitchen sink and then the kitchen sink at him and am sure what guys like you and me living in far civilized times are facing is nothing when compared to what king David faced and went through.But what makes his story recitable after all these hundreds of years is not what he went through, but his going through the tough times and regaining his throne and staying there for 40 years. His comeback in short.

Even better example I would say would be that of Job in Old Testament. See the way life tested him. Am sure, none of you my dear readers were pushed to the limit of trying times Job went through.

I can quote innumerable examples like above. But what ever the legend may be, what ever the history may be, the message from the story is simple and straight forward.

Life tries you sometimes, have faith and a calm mind, lesser you complain lesser the time you will need to get your life back to normalcy. And life has "_ALWAYS_" tried a billionaire far harshly than it did a commoner.

Take sports for example. Some of the greatest games (at least considered to be) to be remembered are those in which one of the player or team makes a strong comeback from a losing position and goes on to win, not the ones which are one sided.

Ivan Lendl defeating John McEnroe in 1984 French open final after trailing 2 sets to nil (That match made me a die hard fan of Ivan Lendl).

India defeating Australia in the famous Eden Garden test in 2001, of course starring VVS Laxman and Rahul Dravid after India being forced in to a follow on.

Mohammad Ali cemented his place in the annals of boxing and more importantly in the hearts of millions due to his legendary comebacks . . . . Both inside and more importantly outside the ring. YES, YES, YES, outside the rings.

All the above anecdotes prove two things. First, that every one is facing down the barrel at some or other juncture of their lives . . . . the juncture may last few hours (Sports) or few years (Politics or Business). Second, it is the refusal of some of the tough individuals to succumb to the "mindset called Defeat" or it is because they *defeated* the "Mindset called defeat" that they escalated themselves to their Status Quo. And notice the phrase "Mindset called defeat". They made sure that they put their mind in their place. And more importantly, they refused to let the mind put them in their place. Almost any Author on self Improvement openly quotes "Defeat is nothing but a mindset". They couldn't be more right.

None other than Mohammad Ali can explain this "Mindset called defeat" better. Read the famous quote from the legendary boxer.

"In the tenth round, suddenly you feel your knuckles burning, your calf muscles spamming, your knees weakening and your mind says "Give up". Defeating *that* voice is really difficult. But, once you do that, defeating your opponent is relatively easy."

In his acclaimed Auto Biography "A Journey" Tony Blair mentions in the chapter "Crisis Management", how he handled the matters with a icy calm(mind). One of the very enlightening sentences from the same chapter is "We are where we were ;we just had to get out of it". Anger or self pity would make the situation more pathetic. As terrific a leader Tony Blair was, the man was incredibly wise. He had to be. He went on to rule a country for a decade.

Take the example of any great man, great sports person or great entrepreneur. They are remarkably calm. Not to say they are cold blooded or insensitive or heartless. As tough as they are, they suffered every negative emotion like self-pity, despondency, helplessness, frustration. Their mettle lied in the fact that they did not succumb to the negative emotions. They kept doing what they had to do despite the negativity . . . both internal and external. "*We are where we were; we just had to get out of it*"

See examples of some of the Tennis greats.

Pete Sampras, Ivan Lendl, Roger Federer, Rafael Nadal . . . the greatest of the greatest tennis players were remarkably rock steady and the results speak for themselves.

Pete Sampras-14 slams (18 slam Finals)

Ivan lendl-8 slams (19 slam finals)

Roger Federer-16 slams (23 Slam Finals)

Rafael Nadal-11 slams (16 slam Finals)

Have you ever seen any of the above players fuming or fretting? I haven't at least. May be the above players did not have the frenzy fan fare like that of Andre Agassi or Boris Becker. But neither Agassi nor Becker(More known for their flamboyance and female following) cannot match the consistent record of the above mentioned players. Maybe the Beckers and the Agassis and the Safins could have a won a lot more but for their incapability to retain their composures in the high pressure situations or when the game swung towards the opponent for a while.

Two of the greatest cricketers world has ever seen Sachin Tendulkar, Rahul Dravid were ice cool through out their careers and their records speak or shall I use the word trumpet for themselves. I have never seen them getting into heated arguments with the worst sledgers of the bowling.

They always "let the bat do the talking" and boy . . . . didn't their bats talk loud!

Bhagavad Gita Ch:12:Verse 15

He for whom no one is put into difficulty and who is not disturbed by anxiety, who is steady in happiness and distress, is very dear to me.

Indeed God seems to be partial to the people who stay calm rather than the ones who get swayed by every up and down that comes their way. The way I have handled myself or rather conditioned myself when ever any thing goes wrong is . . . .

"I am not the first person in the history of mankind to be going through this"

Dear Reader, may be right now, you are hurting or some bitter memory is haunting you or you are reeling from some rude unexpected shock in life. Just accept a simple fact.

"This is life. Such things Happen. Such things can happen to any one"

When I use the word accept, I don't mean surrender or accept defeat with life. What I mean is, grow up, accept the situation as it is instead of complaining or whining and fight your life back. Refusal of even such things happening can lead to major friction in your mind and ruin your composure. Re-quote the sentence by Tony Blair.

"We are where we were; we just had to get out of it"

May be you got dumped by a girl friend . . . . Andre Agassi also got dumped. Yes, the Andre Agassi, the tennis player, over whom females swooned all around the world. And Agassi got dumped when he was already having a Hummer, a corvette and a Viper in his garage. Do guys with Hummers and Corvette get dumped? They do . . . obviously.

May be you lost a job . . . . Steve Jobs got fired from his own company.

May be your business suffered losses . . . . Henry ford was bankrupt twice.

May be your health deteriorated suddenly . . . . Arnold Schwarzenegger (he was on President of USA's fitness council) had a double bypass heart surgery.

May be despite your best efforts there has been some goal you could never achieve and you have to live with the knowledge that you will never get it back . . . . Ivan Lendl never won a Wimbledon despite his grueling preparation. What pains me personally is the fact that he reached Wimbledon finals thrice.

May be someone is hell bent on sabotaging your enterprise . . . . Someone tried to split Bill Gates' Microsoft in to two alleging Bill Gates' Microsoft of monopoly.

May be one of your colleagues is trying to displace you from your coveted designation . . . . Ratan Tata for his first five years at the top had to fight the back stabbers before he cemented himself at the top.

May be some unexpected situation came up from a very unexpected quarters. Tony Blair faced a situation where he had to slaughter loads of livestock suffering from a strange disease, a disease so contagious that it started affecting the rural Britain's tourism. Can it get weirder?

Well guys . . . . that's about everyone's life in some form or another. Some disappointment in one way or another. Some hurdle or other. Some thorn in the flesh, pain in the butt . . . . one way or other. One way or other, life tests you.

But a billionaire is always moving forward. The only difference between the commoner and a billionaire is "A billionaire always uses the same ground he fell on to raise himself". And the most important possession of any billionaire is his **calm mind and his capability to keep it that way.**

So I repeat and you too repeat to yourself . . .

"This is life and such F$%^ing things happen to every body, one way or another. I got to move on" and then *move on.*

Many times the main root cause of self pity is "Why me?" Simple counter argument you can have to yourself is "Such things happen to every one". Believe me guys; there are few stories in the world that have NOT been enacted before. And the moment you realize that, you regain 90% of your composure. Yah . . . . take my word for this . . . . and stop whining, refuse to bow down before the circumstances . . . . buckle up . . . . and keep moving forward. A Billionaire always does or rather Billionaire always is.

(As I write all the above stuff, I cannot agree more on one fact. The fact is "Easier said than done". I know. Believe me, my dear reader, I know. Indeed it is easier said than done. But that's where your true tensile strength is tested. As a great philosopher said "Circumstances don't make you they merely reveal yourself to you")

Having read all the above anecdotes, my dear reader, in case you are thinking that need of calm and strong mind comes only in the times of failure, you couldn't be more wrong. Read again the first three verses mentioned in this chapter.

Bhagavad-Gita Ch.2: Verse 14

O son of kunti, the non permanent appearance of happiness and distress, and their disappearance in due course, are like appearance and dis-appearance of winter and summer seasons. They arise from sense perceptions, O Scion of Bharata, and one must learn to tolerate them without being disturbed.

Bhagavad-Gita Ch.2:Verse 15

O best among men (Arjuna),the person who is not disturbed by happiness and distress and is steady in both is certainly eligible for liberation.

Bhagavad-Gita Ch.2:Verse56

One who is not disturbed in spite of three fold miseries, who is not elated when there is happiness, and who is free from attachment, fear and anger, is called sage of steady mind.

The lord Krishna mentions happiness as boisterously as sadness. Note some of the phrases "Disturbed by happiness" . . . . "not elated when there is happiness"

Surprised? . . . . Weird?? . . . . Strange???

How can one be disturbed by happiness? How can one be not elated in happiness??Answers will come automatically as you read on.

James1:12

Blessed is the man that endureth temptation; for when he is tried, he shall receive the crown of his life, which the lord hath promised to them that love him.

What James meant was . . . .

1. There definitely will be temptations
2. These temptations are definitely going to try your mettle
3. He, who endured these temptations, resists these temptations will be given the promised lands(Both literal and metaphorical).

And what Lord Krishna meant in the above sayings was . . . . in simple terms . . . .

"Don't get carried away. Keep your head firmly above the shoulders and feet firmly on ground. Let not success get into your head". After all, it is easy to be austere when you got nothing to eat.

Trust me, there are as many "Riches to rags" stories as many as "Rags to riches" stories, if you search in Google. Some of the greatest in their field declared bankruptcy. some are alive and some no more. In this section, I 'll refrain from using any names because I know some of the examples I am going to quote, even today have a legion of fans and followers and I don't want to spark any controversy or hurt any one 's feelings. I'll just give a hint and am sure that the readers are smart enough to understand whom am referring to. With all due respect to the hard work, dedication and extreme efforts which helped them to reach the top, I have to mention that once they reached the top, they simply lost their way, lost their mind or were perhaps "disturbed by happiness" or even in more probability "could not endureth temptation".

A famous pop star (the word famous is the mother of understatements) with innumerable records of best selling albums, with a plethora of music awards (Several Grammy awards . . . . many music entertainers dream of one in their life time) and inexhaustible riches (so called inexhaustible) beyond dreams, when dies leaves a debt of more than 300 plus million$. He had everything, name, glamour, money, multi million dollar contracts, fabulous residencies and what not . . . . you name it. He had it. Even the water he took bath with became a talk of the town. World would have died or killed a million times to be him even for a day. But when he dies, he leaves a debt of around 300 million$, not to mention some of the ugly controversies that mired his life. So what went wrong?

Another famous (again . . . the word famous doesn't even come near to describe his fame and frenzy fanfare) music star of the previous generation who had every thing and every thing and everything, in his final days of life needed a gamut of drugs to even fall asleep. Why or how could a guy of such material success suffer from sleeplessness and finally die due to overdose of drugs? Unfathomable . . . . Isn't it? Why should his last days be so pitiable?

A professional boxer, who became the world heavy weight champion at a very tender age, whose legendary punch could have put him on par with Muhammad Ali or a Joe Frazier is today a bankrupt(or has been bankrupt for a while).Not to mention some of the unspeakable controversies and his stint in the prisons several times. Can you believe that some one worth 350 million$ just 2 decades ago goes bankrupt a decade ago. As a matter of fact, when he formally retired from Boxing, one sports columnist writes "you don't deserve a farewell Pete Sampras or Jack Nicholson got. We have retired you out of our hearts long back. You were morally bankrupt long ago". So where did the guy go wrong? Why was a sportsman of such a high caliber given such a scathing farewell?

An Oscar winning Hollywood actor, one of the most highly paid and respected through out the world, recently had his mansions foreclosed and auctioned after being alleged of failure to pay the tax. Why did it happen?

A very famous musician, producer and new pop/soul/rock hybrid pioneer, the funky legend is today living in a van which he parks in some cheap neighborhood in Los Angeles. How the hell did this happen ?

A multi billionaire(Yes a literal billionaire), who was announced the richest man in his country just four years ago and considered to be one of the richest men in Europe just four years ago today(as I write this book) files for bankruptcy. Do such things really happen? Richest man in the country to Bankrupt in a span of four years!

Just type the phrase "Athletes who went broke" in Google and see for yourself how some millionaires (Some of them having in excess of 100 million) in a span of five years had their homes ceased by banks, their yachts confiscated and sadly even their cars were towed away by their creditors. You will be surprised. How can some one spend in excess of 100 million$ in a span of five years? Unfathomable for me at least. But one common thing in all the above stories is.

"They just lost their mind some where down the line. They got disturbed by their happiness, the success just got to their heads or they just stopped using their heads. May be they succumbed to the height of expectations that they themselves have raised. May be they could not resist (endureth) the temptations that comes with the sudden windfall money . . . May be they thought they can get away with anything . . . or who knows perhaps all the above. And eventually they could not reach the "promise land". Or to be more precise, they could not retain the promise land.

Tony Blair speaks in his Autobiography how the expectations he raised among the British public scared the hell out of him once he reached the coveted throne of Prime minister. Of course Tony Blair handled his expectations exceptionally well and he is definitely not one of the examples I quoted in the second half of this chapter. His ten years at the top more than proves it.

Talking about riches to raggers, may be they got carried away by success, may be they thought they can just get away with any thing, may be they made some foolish decisions. In one of the above examples, I mentioned a richest guy in the country who files for bankruptcy. All the business analysts agree unanimously on one thing. He put all the eggs in one basket. The basket collapsed and along with it went all his eggs.

The moral is "**their mind just ceased to be calm and composed once they reached a certain level of success**".

One funnier thing (OK not so funny) I observed is, many of the guys who went broke went so because of multiple expensive divorces. Do you see a pattern here?

I see and hope you agree with it. Successful people have successful, long lasting and more often ever lasting relationships. Successful businessmen, successful sportsmen, for that matter successful men in any field have steady relations.

See the list of examples I quote below.

Bill Gates married Melinda French on January 1, 1994 and they had a rock steady marriage for almost last 2 decades and they are going strong.

Carlos Slim was married to Soumaya Domit from 1967 until her death in 1999.

Warren Buffet's marriage with Susan Buffet lasted for more than 50 years.

Laxmi Mittal has been married to Usha Mittal for more than 30 years.

In movie field, where philandering is considered another day in the office, some of the greatest actors had some seriously long term relations.

Amitabh Bachchan, the legendary Indian actor has been married to a single woman for almost 4 decades.

Shahrukh khan, addressed as King Khan, living legend has been married to the same female for almost two decades. Not a single gossip, not a single link up with any co star, not a single "the other woman" controversy in his illustrious career.

Sachin Tendulkar, the cricketing legend, who signed a 25 million$ contract with Adidas at the age of 25, got married to his teenage crush at the age of 21 in 1994.And that's the way it stays till date. And I have no doubt, that's the way it is gonna stay till . . . .

The above mentioned gentlemen are among the world's richest and most successful people. They could have had anything (anyone) they want. But the self control and the discipline they exercised is there for the world to see. Does it a ring a bell? Are all of you seeing some correlation between a successful relation and a successful prosperous life? I do and hope you too do. And all of you won't have absolutely any problem in agreeing that a steady long term relation does need a *calm mind*. Contrary to the common opinion that a successful relationship leads to a calm mind, the fact is calm mind leads to a successful relationship. Surely a guy who lets his mind sway by every inconvenient act of his partner just cannot have a long enduring relationship. Arnold Schwarzenegger as astute as he was makes a very interesting note.

"Successful relation enriches your life"

Agree with Arnold? I couldn't agree more. And indeed successful relation does need a calm mind. Any grownup adult knows it for sure.

Getting back to the importance of a calm mind, calm men have remarkably prosperous life, both personal and professional . . . . fair and square truth.

This whole chapter I devoted to the importance of a calm mind. I hope all my dear readers also understand the importance of calm mind to achieve your goals and why it is even more important to have a calm, composed mind after you reach the top. I also hope all of you get a glimpse of the destructive capacity of a disturbed mind. A calm mind can take you to celestial heights and a disturbed mind can take you to pathetic, abysmal lows.

The higher the goals you have, the stronger, the calmer, the more rigid mind (Don't mistake rigid with adamant . . . please) you need. And Billionaires always, yes always and always and always are equipped with an immovable rock steady mind. They have to be . . . No other go.

Bhagavad Gita: Chapter 6: Verse 6
For him who has conquered mind, the mind is the best of friends; but for one who has failed to do so; his very mind will be the greatest enemy.

Does the above verse sum it all the importance of having a controlled mind?

James Allen, the foremost western expounder of importance of having a controlled mind explains in his all time classic "As a man thinketh" (A must read book for every one in this world) has dedicated an entire book on the importance of calm mind. In one of his chapters he preaches that Calmness of mind is one of the beautiful jewels of wisdom. Highest of the wisdom indeed descends upon the calmest of the mind. It is not for nothing elders say "Calm down" in the times of adversity.

> "To the dull mind, all nature is leaden. To the illumined mind the whole world burns and sparkles with light"—**Ralph Waldo Emerson**.

I honestly don't know whether Emerson read Bhagavad-Gita or not. Of course, no one needs to be surprised if somebody as erudite as Emerson has read Bhagavad-Gita several times. But does what Emerson said echo with what Lord Krishna said several, several centuries ago?

More I observe human beings, more it appears to be true. The same situation, the same environment, the same surrounding, the same incident . . . . a person with wise, optimistic, illumined mind reacts in a certain way, another with an ignorant, pessimistic, darkened mind reacts in another way. Where ignorant mind sees a problem, wise mind sees a challenge, where a pessimistic mind sees a hurdle; optimistic mind sees a stepping stone. Where a darkened mind sees a closed door, an illumined mind sees a new door opening. Trust me. This is not some self improvement rhetoric. It's a fact.

When one sees a millionaire athlete go broke in span of five years, most of the people see a cheap joke or gossip column, but a wise man sees a lesson he should never forget. Arnold Schwarzenegger, in his Autobiography explains candidly how he saw several contemporary athletes and entertainers driving Rolls-Royce one day and declaring bankruptcy the other day. He looked into their lives, saw the mistake they did (For eg. delegating all finances to a manager, and giving a hoot to money matters) and most importantly implemented the lessons he learnt from other's lives. Does the Ex-Mr.Olympia reflect the below saying?

"Smart men learn from their mistakes,
Wise learn from other's mistakes".

One person suffers the Nazi atrocities(Anyone who has a decent knowledge of 2nd world war knows how unspeakably horrible the atrocities were) and becomes a depressed human being for rest of their life and waits for the end. One person strengthens his belief in his creator and sets himself as an example to the rest of mankind to show that even most repugnant of the external conditions have a reason, a purpose, a lesson,provided you are wiling to seek. There is one last boundary which no one can conquer i.e., your mind. Of course, the later person I am referring to is Viktor Frankl. Viktor Frankl proclaimed to the whole world "Everything is indeed in your mind".

Receiving an insult, one man feels sad and one man feels enraged. And when that rage is experienced by a Charismatic millionaire cum tractor manufacturer called Lombargini Ferrucio, the reaction or rather output of the reaction is the Iconic car "Lombargini".Story goes something like this. Ferrucio Lamborghini owned a Ferrari which later had a clutch trouble. When he approached Enzo Ferrari with some suggestions, Ferrari dismissed him on the lines of something like "what does a Tractor manufacturer know about Sports cars. Leave the sports cars to me and mind your tractors". Well, the rest as they say is history. Lamborghini started manufacturing of car with a logo resembling a raging bull on its face and that Lamborghini car is even today giving Ferrari a run for its money.

Yes . . . . reading Ayn Rand's all time classic "Atlas Shrugged" will not do any help to some one narrow minded. On the other hand, I have seen guys who ridiculed "Atlas Shrugged" and "Fountain Head" as huge waste of time. Well . . . . What a shame!!

After Listening to Speech of Narayan Murthy, the elderly statesman of Indian business community, one guy feels bored, other guy feels inspired. Trust me. I had the privilege of meeting both the guys. So what exactly do you infer?

And shall I give you a funny example? Am sure the below example is gonna bring a smile to your face.

Remember your school bell? School bell at morning 9 am brings a frown to your face, but school bell at evening 4 pm is going bring smiles and grins on your face. How vividly I remember peeking at my Seiko watch (the first watch my father gifted to me) from 3pm in the afternoon during my school days!! But I hope my dear readers are getting the point.

The list can go on and on and on . . . . But my dear readers, I hope you get the point. It is not what happens outside which shapes your identity, but what your mind interprets out of it and more importantly how your mind reacts to the outer circumstances which shapes your life. I am sure you heard the last sentence before. And now with the above examples in your mind, read the below verse again very carefully.

Bhagavad-Gita Ch.2: Verse 14

O son of kunti, the non permanent appearance of happiness and distress, and their disappearance in due course, are like appearance and dis-appearance of winter and summer seasons. They arise from sense perceptions, O Scion of Bharata, and one must learn to tolerate them without being disturbed.

Happiness and Sadness arise from sense perceptions. And I am going to add, more sensible you are, the better perception or evaluation you extract (takeaway) from a given input of life. Wiser your mind, better you can interpret the world. Wiser and more matured your mind, better your evaluation of the incident that happened. Wisdom comes partly from experience, partly by carefully observing others, majorly by reading some great books and most importantly, how willing you are to have an open, wise mind. Of course nothing can replace the wisdom that comes with age. You have to grow for that.

Well, have I given enough examples to demonstrate the importance of calm, controlled wise mind? If any one is still thinking, because that happened to me, I am like that, because this happened to me, I am like this, I hope they are reconsidering their stance. What they are or where they have reached is nothing but the reaction & perception of **their own** minds to the external conditions.

One of the most pre-eminent philosopher and intellectuals of early twentieth Century Aldous Huxley said the below.

"Experience is not what happens to a man, but it is what a man does with what happens to him".

And needless to say, the wiser your mind is, the more the number of options you have to pick and best of the option you pick.

Bhagavad Gita: Chapter 6: Verse 5

A man must elevate himself by his own mind,
not degrade himself. The mind is the friend of
the conditioned soul and his enemy as well.

"It's not good enough to have a good mind, the main
thing is to use it well"-**Rene Descartes** (Yah . . . . the same
mathematician who developed the Cartesian plane, X
coordinates . . . . Y coordinates . . . .).

Does the sixteenth century ace mathematician second
what Lord Krishna said looooong back? It appears so. A
guy who developed the entire Cartesian plane, the linear,
polynomial way of expressing the position of any given point
in the universe indeed must have used his mind well . . . . to
say the least. He had one hell of a friend . . . . his mind. Any
arguments ? Hope not.

Bhagavad Gita: Chapter 6: Verse 36

For whose mind is unbridled, self realization is
difficult work. But he whose mind is controlled
and who strives by the right means is assured of
Success.

Read the later sentence once again.

"But he whose mind is controlled and who strives by the right means is assured of Success"

Without a controlled mind, self realization is difficult.
Even realizing your own self, understanding your own
self, your own personality, your own mentality, your own
strengths and weaknesses will be difficult with out a well
controlled mind, let alone achieving the goals given by higher

self. With out a calm mind realizing the right means for a goal is difficult to say the least. Many a times, it turns out the means to a certain goal you select in a negative (angry, desperate, depressed, carried away, arrogant) frame of mind may be productive in short term, but many a times it proves detrimental or counter productive in the long term. I am sure anyone can find several examples, where some one became rich through the wrong means and ended up in a mess (prison, public shame).Surely that is not the kind of success I have been alluding to all the way.

One particular Politician in India who misused his power to earn thousands of millions of rupees through a massive scam is today in a prison. He brazenly displayed his wrongly earned wealth; Dining chairs and table were made of gold. He used to sit on a golden throne in his home and talk to press. Talk of arrogance! And today he eats food served in a cheap aluminum plate in a place which is five feet away from toilet. His eating place and defecating place are separated by a two and a half feet high wall. Am sure, none of you readers want success of this kind. Do you? Nope, not at all. I wanted to give you an example of so called success achieved through wrong means and its later ramifications.

And the right means hormonal to highest ethics and morals can be suggested to you **ONLY** by a calm mind.

James Allen in his all time classic "As a man thinketh" clearly says "Go into silence at least an hour a day and implement what instructions come out of your calm mind. The path given by your calm mind will be harmonious with your self and will be in harmony with the highest ethics".

How you control your mind is well beyond the scope of this book. Hundreds of schools of mind control, yoga, meditation have sprouted around the world. Well, dear reader, you can join any yoga Guru's school, read books written by many enlightened masters, any religious head. There are several means to control your mind. World has increasingly acknowledged the importance of Yoga, breathing exercise, Japa, observing thoughts, meditation in this busy, competitive, hectic world.

So friends . . . . mind your mind . . . . Always. Nope, this is not a suggestion. It is a command given by the celestial masters.

And as if enough has not been already said about the importance of calm mind, one final nail in the coffin, one final corroboration from James, the Servant of Jesus Christ . . . .

James 1:8
A double minded man is unstable in all his ways.

Enough of extolling a calm mind and criticizing an unstable mind!

COURAGE, FEARLESSNESS, BRAVADO, AUDACITY, GUTS, SAME THING . . . . SEVERAL NAMES

(Before I go ahead, I must mention that it took me some time to decide which chapter I should put forth first . . . . belief or courage . . . . does belief come out of courage or courage comes out of belief . . . . the debate can go on, on& on . . . . So I cautiously chose belief first . . . .)

The word courage may immediately bring to your mind Sylvester Stallone a.k.a John Rambo taking on dozens of Spetznaz commandoes in the Afghan territory and single handedly killing them all without a bullet scratch(ok . . . . may be a scratch) or a Jackie Chan jumping from a three storied building on to a moving bus. Indeed it does take more than courage for a commando to walk into enemy territory or to perform those mind boggling stunts (Jackie Chan is one of my all time favorite actors),but Courage necessarily does not mean only that.

Courage is as much as a pre-requisite as a calm mind for success. Take any book on leadership, take any book on success, this quality called courage definitely ranks among the top three qualities in the author's list. Chapter on courage is as surely there as the chapter on self-belief. Courage and belief very much go hand in hand. Courage comes out of Self belief, Self belief comes out courage. Courage simply put means "A strong belief in your self that you are capable of facing any circumstance which may come your way without losing your composure and calm mind . . . . A strong belief in your self that you can hit back at life if and when(*When* is perhaps more appropriate than *if)* life hits you. "Well, easier said than done" . . . . you may say. Indeed easier said than done. But then again, becoming a billionaire is not an easy task either.

Bhagavad Gita Ch:16 verse 1-3

The blessed lord said: fearlessness, purification of one's existence, enhancement of the spiritual knowledge, charity, self-control, performance of sacrifice, studying Vedas, austerity and simplicity; non violence, truth-fullness, freedom from anger, renunciation, tranquility, aversion to fault finding, compassion and freedom from cunningness, gentleness, modesty and steady determination; vigor, forgiveness, fortitude, cleanliness, freedom from envy and the passion for honor—these transcendental qualities son of Bharata, belong to godly men endowed with divine nature.

Read all the above qualities carefully and let each quality seep into your mind as deeply as possible and then you observe any billionaire. Some or other quality mentioned in the above list is present in every billionaire in higher or lower degree. Some billionaires may have some qualities and some may have others. Some of the above divine mentioned qualities may be totally absent also in some of them. After all, Billionaires are also human beings. So, may be they have had their deficiencies. But one quality which *every* billionaire must be having is . . . . **Courage.** Mind you . . . . I don't use the word "every" loosely. I really mean "Every". Do you know one coward billionaire? Take any field . . . . yes, yes, yes . . . . any field.

Business . . . . art . . . . science . . . . philosophy . . . sport . . . . Politics . . . . humanatarian service . . . . or Money making for that matter. Robert Kiyosoki, the self made millionaire, more famous for his book "Rich Dad and Poor Dad" very rightly said "Riches are not meant for Cowards".

Can some one point out one billionaire or towering personality in his respective field who lacked courage? Who happens to be a coward? Some one please . . . . nope you just cannot.

And what is the first divine quality which lord Krishna mentioned as divine?

Answer: Fearlessness (Refer to the above verse).

Does it say anything about the paramount importance of this quality called fearlessness, courage, guts, nerves, balls (okay that's bit slang)? But, hope you are getting a feel of it.

Like any self improvement seeker, I read several classics about self improvement. The three classic books I have read several times and am going to read several more times are *Magic of thinking Big* by David Schwartz, *The Power of Positive Thinking* by Dr.Norman Vincent Peale and *Think and Grow Rich* by Napoleon Hill. All the three authors have laid extreme emphasis on how to conquer fear. Napoleon Hill, most of all. He devoted the biggest and the last chapter about how to conquer your fears. No author cauterized this weakness called Fear as much as he did. Fear Kills imagination. Fear kills enthusiasm. Fear kills initiative. Fear kills your personality . . . . , fear kills . . . . fear kills . . . . fear kills . . . . fear kills. Hill goes on and on and on. Hill goes on candidly to say that all the techniques he taught in all the previous chapters of his book are a sheer waste if you are overpowered by one weakness called Fear.

In one of my previous chapters I mentioned about one retired gentlemen who spent more than 2 decades in a department he did not like to work in just because he could not muster enough courage to ask his boss to change his department. More than 20 years doing what he did not like to do!! Can there be a limit for helplessness and cowardice? And I hope my readers can see the magnitude of damage and misery this weakness called fear can bring into our lives.

Swami Parmahansa Yogananda in one of his famous lectures declares openly that fear is the biggest enemy of will power. He goes on to say that fear is the force that saps out your will power and re-iterates that courage is our birth right. And of course fear is a satanic property. It takes you away from God.

Courage has several definitions.

But one definition which has always inspired me is "Courage does not mean absence of fear. Courage means deciding that doing the right thing is more important than succumbing to fear and then doing it".

I first heard of King David, arguably the second most famous personality in the entire bible when I was, may be seven or eight years old. The story of course is about David's confrontation with the Giant Goliath. How he, as a boy used nothing but a sling and one smooth stone to kill the giant and went on to decapitate Goliath with Goliath's own sword. As an eight year old boy, perhaps I did not fathom the magnitude of moral in the story. But today as a 34 year old, I indeed realize that facing the Goliaths of life is easier than not. Agree? In case you disagree, let me tell all you one fact of life. If you want to be a billionaire, you are going to face lots of Goliaths enroute and its going to take much more than a sling and a smooth stone to kill them.

As I thought of some personalities whom I can quote as examples, almost all the personalities I mentioned in the chapter.2(the one about Self Belief) fit as much in this chapter as in that chapter. Please revert back to that chapter and go through the examples & personalities I mentioned. Can you point out one person who lacked courage? And mind you, as I went on to observe the lives of the super successful, I couldn't help observing one very inspiring fact. They displayed (read needed) higher level of courage after they reached the top rather than when they started on the not so beaten path. Yah, it's a fact. They faced bigger Goliaths after they became more successful. They had to. That's very contradictory to the common opinion that billionaires have a rosy life for whom life is served on a platter.

As Pete Sampras, the nonchalant tennis player says "Its *after* you reach the top, every one paints a bulls eye on your back". Be prepared.

See the below personalities who refused to succumb to fear and who kept going forward despite the gamut of obstacles and conspirators. Ordinary mortals can't even imagine being in their shoes.

Ratan Tata, *after* he became the Chairman of Tata Sons faced a gamut of obstacles and problems from some very high profile politicians, some very powerful labor unions and more importantly some fierce enmity from very influential satraps of some of his own group companies who tried to topple him of the top position. Not only did Ratan Tata face one Goliath after another, he eliminated all of them one by one and established a conglomerate whose heights have become unreachable by any business house in

India, at least in near future. Especially the saga of Ratan Tata's releasing into the market the world smallest car, Nano (Price 0.1 million Rupees)! A politician almost jeopardized the project by starting the land issue after the entire assembly plant was laid and manufacturing of the car almost started. The deftness and decisiveness Ratan Tata showed with his overnight decision to shift the entire plant to a new location in a totally different state of India and releasing the Nano "On time" left the whole world gaping at him. And of course the criticisms he faced from the whole world after he released the car into the Market. "The car is a golf cart etc etc" . . . . Phew!!!! Where is the limit for courage and endurance a man need to posses? Can there be a greater example of "Never say die" attitude. But then again, world hasn't seen many Ratan Tatas either.

Bill Gates took on the Government of United states (Goliath) head on when some body tried to divide his Microsoft into two accusing him of monopoly. Not to mention the number of law suits accusing him of this, accusing him of that. Well, how many of the accusations are true . . . . lets not go into that. But one simple fact, which is nothing new to mankind, which gets reiterated is "every super successful human being is targeted by lesser myopic men". It does take more than guts to take them on and to win over them.

Chatrapati Shivaji, the pride and founder of Maratha Empire took on the mighty Moghul Empire (Goliath) single handedly. Saying he was courageous is preposterous. He not only took on the might of the Aurangzeb, the then emperor of the Moghul Kingdom but also established an empire which remained unshakable for several forth coming generations. In case anyone is not acquainted with Indian history, please note that at that time Shivaji was a leader of a small province in South west India and Aurangzeb was ruling an empire which prevailed from the southern most part of the country to the the northern most.

Indira Gandhi, one of the most influential Prime Ministers of India, took on an entire powerful Sikh community when she ordered Operation Blue Star; the controversial operation which lead to her own demise. Irrespective of the output, it took tons and tons of courage to do what she did. Opinions differ about her ordering the Operation. But one unanimous opinion is, it took guts to go ahead with the military operation.

Winston Churchill, who led the British to victory in the Second World War, features in almost any article I read about courage. His launching counter attack against Nazis and more importantly the way he carried the nation on his shoulders through the incredibly tough 5-6 years in the British history will remain an epitome of courage in the annals of history. How can a man live with himself when he knows his decision can make the difference between life and death of millions of his soldiers (and their families)? What strength of heart should man posses to shoulder responsibly of such magnitude? Well, no doubt, Winston Churchill has cemented his name in the history books as the greatest British Prime minister ever.

Narayan Murthy, the founder of Infosys, took on the might of IBM when he started his Infosys along with six partners. Courage? . . . . Of course Courage. It was only a matter of time Infosys became the first Indian company to be listed in NASDAQ. After Narayan Murthy became the business icon of India, some petty politicians started taking pot shots at him. He not only gave them a fitting reply, but made sure, no lesser men even thinks about passing any negative remarks at him. Five years after his retirement, the board of directors asked him to re-take the reins of the company to regain the sheen, the company lost after his retirement. Does that say anything about the man's mettle? It doesn't say. It screams!!!

Thomas J Watson Sr, founder of IBM, as much as a visionary businessman he was, he let the world know what steel of a **man** he was, when he refused to sell any IBM machines to the Nazi Germany during the second world war. He was willing to take the ire of Adolf Hitler for sake of principles he believed in! Can there be a higher testimony of a character called Courage. Sheer Audacity I would say. One famous quote from Sir Thomas J Watson is "If you keep doing what you fear, eventually fear will meet its death". Well, the great man lived by his principles, didn't he?

The courage Ross Perrot, the independent presidential candidate for United states of America in the year 1992, displayed when he sponsored an armed forces raid in Iran (Goliath) for sake his two employees remains unparelled. It isn't an understatement to say that he took on an entire community when he did what he did. His becoming a billionaire (literally) should not surprise anyone. His establishing data processing company with an investment of 1000 dollars and his being 101st richest American looks very natural in hindsight. Armed with that magnitude of courage, what cannot a man do??

Aung San Syu Kyi, the Burmese activist on whom awards & rewards from all over the world have been bestowed upon is one of my favorite and inspiring stories of courage and indomitable spirit. A puny 5 foot 5 inch woman takes on the might of a ruthless totalitarian junta. And world knows how long she fought despite years of house arrest and what not unmentionable humiliations. For 21 years! From where did this woman muster the courage and strength to persevere for

21 years? And today democracy is promised in Burma. Am sure her story of willpower is going to inspire generations of mankind to say the least. And can the world see how the biggest of the adversities bow down in front of one word "Courage". Sheer unbreakable courage!

Jesus Christ did not give a hoot about the wrath he was going to suffer in the hands of the Roman Empire. He went about doing the job assigned to him in a clean professional way. Audacity? Could not think of better word. Does English vocabulary have a word to describe the magnitude of courage Jesus Christ possessed? Not that I know of. And God knows and every one agrees that till the sun and moon remain, what Jesus manifested is going to stay. Irrespective of the different opinions of different pastors and preachers, my personal interpretation from Jesus's life story is "if you don't have courage to carry your cross on your shoulders, take a couple of whiplashes on your back, thorn crown on your head and of course even willing to be even crucified for sake of what you believe, there is no chance of redemption and of course resurrection into the supreme". Am sure my readers can understand the above metaphor. Trust me friends, all the billionaires were crucified (of course, not nailed to the Cross literally ☺) partially at least at one or another point of their life.

The above examples conclusively conclude what a courageous human being is capable of manifesting.

Life is a daring adventure or nothing-Helen Keller

Well, let's ask ourselves . . . are we really daring to do something big or are we one among the crowds that walk in the crowded street? You know the answer my dear reader, only you can know. Are we willing to go to the edge of the cliff at some point of your life? Are you willing to walk on the tight rope at least once in a while? Are you willing to feel the risk at some point of life? Are you willing to spend some sleepless nights? If the answer is "Yes" then indeed you are capable of something big. Believe me, something big is very much round the corner. All you have to do is persevere and see yourself through.

If not, most probably you are one of those **secure** job holders who is quite content with their mediocre life . . . . ok may be upper middle class . . . . ok may be reasonably rich. But if you want to be a billionaire, in the sense I have been using the word all through the book, well, you must dare. You must dare step into unbeaten path some time or other. At least for a while. There is no other choice.

Proverbs 29:18

"Where there is no vision; people perish . . . ."

Every billionaire has a vision. A very unique vision; and they backed their vision to the hilt with immeasurable determination, immeasurable belief and of course undaunting perseverance & courage. Observe carefully the vision of every visionary. It does not take a genius to figure out that it takes some real magnitude of courage to even envision their visions in their contemporary times not to mention the brazenly bold steps they took.

Swami Paramahansa Yogananda came (went . . . . depending on whether you are reading this book in America or India) to United States of America in 1920s when not many even heard of the word "Hinduism". He went to USA with a clear vision of bringing the orient (east) and occident (West) together through a bridge called Yoga or spirituality. He took on the obstacles that came his way in the stride; the myopic people who would prevent the popularity of the yoga &his teachings, the jealous people who did false propaganda against him. It took almost 35 years of his life (35 years!!) to achieve his goal. Not many would debate that today's popularity of the word "yoga" in the west can be credited to one man, Swami Yogananda Paramahansa. And of course his autobiography "Autobiography of a Yogi" (A must read for any Spiritual seeker) is an all time classic. Recently I came across an article which said some inmates in a French prison got into a brawl about who is going to read the book first! How's that for popularity of a spiritual book? How's that for influence of a man's teachings?

Copernicus envisioned a solar system in which the Sun is at the center and the planets revolving around them. In his contemporary times, when what ever church said was the gospel, he not only put forward his theory, but also stood by it. Well, it is sad that he did not get the recognition he so well deserved during his life time. At least, history has acknowledged his greatness.

Anand Mahindra, Chairman of the Mahindra Rise group, recalls the sleepless nights (nearly 2 years) he spent before launching the iconic MUV Mahindra Scorpio. Before the launch of the "Scorpio", Mahindra and Mahindra (Now Mahindra Rise) was a mediocre third world country automobile company manufacturing some very ordinary looking jeeps and tractors? As a matter of fact, some of his "friends" advised him to dispose of the automotive sector of the group quoting Indian liberalization and advent of number of foreign automobile companies into the country as a reason. But it was the courage and vision (and an investment of nearly 6000 million rupees) of one man, Anand Mahindra (the then vice Chairman), which lead to the genesis of Scorpio using the state of art fuel pump technology (Common rail diesel injection) and revamping of the very image of the group. Today all the vehicles that roll out of the Mahindra Rise group have an air of modernization on par with any leading SUV in the world . . . . Waiting time at almost every dealership is nearly ten months. Hardly any VVIP (Including that of Prime Minister) convoy in India with out a Scorpio!! Does it say something about the efficacy of the vehicle? And power of one man's indomitable courage and unflinching vision.

Every billionaire at some or other juncture of his life did dare. It's an irrefutable fact. At some or other point of his life, he must have taken a deep breath and must have **gone for it**. He must have taken the plunge, leapt the leap of faith, call it what ever you want to. He did it fully knowing that there were going to be some choke points, bottle necks and bruises (Financial, Emotional) waiting for him. All the billionaires at some juncture did put something in the line of fire . . . . perhaps, their reputations, their money, their comfort, their sleep and some dare devils, even their lives (Jackie Chan puts his life on line consistently for sake of those daredevil stunts. Every one knows how highly regarded he is through out the world and of course his Guinness book record "Maximum number of stunts by a living person" says it all).

Many people whom I have interviewed had a very similar answer when I asked them a common question. The question was "how come you did not go for it when you knew you wanted it?" The similar answer was "I did not know if I could achieve it. I did not know how things will turn out. I was not sure, I had a wife & kid to take care of, so I could not risk . . . . etc. etc." When I retaliated how they knew they cannot do if they never even tried, they just didn't have any answer. The answer is simple. They just did not have courage to go ahead.

A couple of analogies I would like to give here before I go further. Take the example of swimming. You can hire best of the coaches. Best of the swimming coaches can teach all the theories about how to swim "Take breath at regular intervals . . . . rotate the hands like this . . . . flap your legs like this . . . . balance your neck like that . . . . blah . . . . blah . . . . blah". But can you learn to swim unless you jump into the water, get choked in the water a couple of times, feel the water abruptly enter your nostrils a couple of times, cough your lungs out a couple of times? Can you?

Can you learn to ride the bicycle without bruising elbows and knees a couple of times? As 10 year old kids, we were not afraid of the bruises and scratches. How many times did we get our elbow bruised before we perfected the bicycle? Did the bruise deter us from trying to ride the bicycle the next time? Of course not.

But as we grew up, we got acquainted with the "realities" of life. Didn't we? Indeed we did. We become afraid of the bruises and scars. Perhaps emotional. Perhaps financial. Perhaps social. Where did that child like enthusiasm go? It is very much right there . . . . within us. All we need to do is to bring out the same child like enthusiasm and the same childish courage which is capable of overwhelming all our fears. And yes, that courage is right within us. The courage to take a step into the unknown, the courage to explore the unexplored frontiers of world (disregarding the choke points and the hurdles) . . . . yes, yes, yes . . . . its right there in you.

One of the Winston Churchill famous quotes is

"Courage is nothing but going from one failure to other failure without losing enthusiasm".

That non-losing enthusiasm mentality is right within us. It is we, who should manifest the same enthusiasm.

Revelations 21:8

But the fearful, and the unbelieving and the abominable, and murderers, and the whore mongers, and sorcerers and idolaters, and all liars shall have their part in the lake which burneth with fire and brimstone: which is the second death.

Read the above revelation. The fearful and the unbelieving will be . . . . Second death.

See the two words, the unbelieving and the fearful. Both shall be cauterized. Do the above two words re-emphasize the importance of the two most important qualities a human being must have. Courage and belief. And more importantly, did the above revelation reveal to you in a metaphorical manner, what fate awaits people who lack both belief and courage (***shall have their part in the lake which burneth with fire and brimstone: which is the second death***)?

A saying in Telugu (My mother Tongue language) goes on to say . . . .

"A courageous man dies only once, a coward dies 1000 times again and again".

Does the above saying play a second fiddle to what was said in the above revelation? Hope you agree my dear readers.

Swami Vivekananda said in one of his lectures "Fear is sin, fear is wrong way of life. If anyone tries to scare you and you get scared, it is you who has sinned".

All throughout Bhagavad-Gita, what did lord Krishna tell Arjuna?

"Don't succumb to your despondency. Take up your weapon into your hands and fight. If you don't fight, history & your enemies will dismiss you as a coward. Dis-honor and ill—fame are going to haunt you. It's going to be worse than death".

Bhagavad Gita Ch2: Verse 3

O Son of Partha, do not yield to this degrading impotence. It does not become you. Give up such petty weakness of heart and arise, O chastiser of the enemy

Living in cowardice is worse than death. Succumbing to fear is the first step which leads to "unbecoming of you". Having said that, I must admit that during all my school & college life, I have been a timid guy myself. But one incident made me realize that living courageously is *actually easier* than living in cowardice.

There was a guy in college who constantly used to tease me. Being timid I always oppressed my anger. I just could not muster enough courage to vent out my anger. But in one incident, that fellow crossed the line between teasing and insulting. That day I got so enraged I went to his room in the hostel and picked a very serious fight with him. Hadn't others intervened and pulled us apart, things would have gone physical. Had it gone physical, I would have most probably lost the fight. That fellow had a fair 7 inches height over me. I remember the incident very vividly and the name of the guy. But I'll neither mention the details nor the name of the guy. But what happened later was a profound lesson I learnt and will remember for rest of my life. *That guy never messed with me again*. More importantly, no one else messed with me again. As a matter of fact, he started apologizing for even accidental brush of shoulder in the dorm. The lesson was "face your fears and fear will run away from you". For a long time, I thought I picked up the fight with that guy. But what later dawned to me was I picked up the fight with my own fear. Once I won over that fear, fighting the 7 inch taller guy was relatively easy. I clearly realized that ability to fight fear i.e., Courage was there in me . . . . latent. It had to come out some day and it did.

Am sure all my readers have a very similar memory. Am sure all of you had heard the dialogue from some one or other "I myself didn't know from where I got that guts that day". Well the answer is "the guts were right there inside him/her". So I encourage you my dear friends, in case you are wondering from where you can muster the courage to "go for it", to aim for something big, to follow your heart, or to try to reach for the sky . . . . just believe in something "the needed courage is right there in side you".

Lord Krishna himself assured so clearly that he will make up for the deficiencies *as long as you keep trying.* I am sure you can understand why I mentioned "as long as you keep trying" in italics . . . . importance of working . . . . third chapter.

Bhagavad-Gita Chapter 9: verse 22

"To men who meditate on me as their very own
ever united to me by incessant worship, I supply
their deficiencies and make permanent gains"

So why do you need to fear? The lord said he would give you what you need at the needed time. Perhaps even courage. Providence knows.

I am sure any one with half decent knowledge of Bhagavad Gita must have heard of the arguably most famous sentence in Bhagavad Gita from Karma Yoga.

"Do your best and leave your best to me.Its just not your duty to worry about your result. I dispatch the result. Fear is nothing but anxiety or worry about the result".

Bhagavad Gita Ch:2 Verse 47
You have a right to perform your prescribed duty, but you are not entitled to the fruits of action. Never consider yourself to be the cause of the results of your activities, and never be attached to not doing your duty

Bhagavad Gita Ch:2 Verse 48
Be steadfast in yoga, O Arjuna, Perform your duty and abandon all attachment to success or failure.Such evenness of mind is called yoga.

Now see what Lord Jesus Christ says in the first chapter of New Testament.

Mathew 6:34
Take no thought for morrow; for morrow shall take thoughts for the things itself.

Do the above sayings encourage you my dear readers? Stress relieving? It did for me atleast. Do what is needed to be done today and tomorrow shall fall in to place by itself the dear lord says. And I trust in his words. I have decided to go by faith and act in the name of faith. And friends, you too have courage to do what you want to do.

When I first read the above sayings I must agree that I was skeptical. How can you not worry about the result? How can you not worry about what is in store for tomorrow. After all, tomorrow is definitely going to become today in another 24 hours. But as I went about reading the lives of billionaires, I couldn't help understanding that indeed all billionaires have taken a leap of faith. They took the jump because they had to and that's what they had to do at that juncture. They refused to worry about the result. They refused to be anxious about tomorrow. As a matter of fact, it seems to be mere common sense. Understanding the above sayings from a higher perspective gave me a new meaning and I am going to share that meaning with you.

The meaning is "the quality of the efforts and the work you do will get negatively affected if you are worrying about the result. You will not be able to work with the same positive frame of mind and unbridled enthusiasm if you were worrying about the output that awaits you tomorrow". So do your best, what you ought to do today with whole and sole concentration and let providence deliver the commensurate results. Trust me friends . . . . HE WILL.

A lesson which Pete Sampras learned in his early phase of his career!! After his first Grand slam victory, US Open 1990, he started playing every tournament *just to win*. With nothing but victory & trophy on his mind. He went on for 3 years without a Grand Slam win. And upon introspection, he found that his constantly thinking about winning another grand slam was putting intolerable stress and unbearable tension in him. More importantly, he realized that his eagerness and impatience to win was getting to his nerves and affecting his game negatively. And naturally, he went on without a Grand slam win for another 3 years. Surely, but steadily he realized the wisdom "play your best tennis one point after one point after one point and let the match unfold in its natural course". And world just gaped at him as he won slam after slam after slam till Roger Federer came along ushering a new era. And when a guy who won 14 grand slams abided by a "code" during his glittering career, there must be some efficacy in his code.

Mahatma Gandhi started his non violence movement and went about in clean professional way. Was he ever ever worried about the result? Ever? And what was he confronting? The British Empire. The empire in which Sun never set!! Atleast in those days! He started the movement because he had to. He believed in his means and went on to do his job. Did he ever complain how long it is going to take? Has history recorded any impatience from Gandhi? The one and only thing he concentrated was what he had to do "now". Mahatma Gandhi all through his life used two books for guidance. Well, no prizes for guessing. The Bible and Bhagavad-Gita.

One more self made Billionaire, Jeff Peros the founder of Amazon is a classic example of patience, doing your best and leaving the result to unfold by itself. For six years,Amazon worked on wafer thin margins. But Jeff Peros always concentrated on the customer satisfaction, his company's prime motto. And such patience does indeed come only when you concentrate on the work in the hand rather than worrying about the result. Oh yeah . . . . trust me. And he today (as I write this book) is worth a cool 24 billion dollars. Does it proclaim to the world the efficacy of the "do your best and leave the rest to above" policy?

And ofcourse, the example of Bill gates who offered the BASIC software to one company when he had not yet developed it. He not only committed that he is going to deliver,but he also negotiated the terms of contract. One of the terms of contract was that he should be able to license the software to any other company he wants. Well, as they say, rest is history. Saying Bill Gates changed the world is an understatement. He was a billionaire even before he was thirty years old. But I hope all my dear readers understand the brash audacity of Bill Gates and the correctness of the policy "doing what needs to be done today without taking a thought for tomorrow". Many would question the ethicality of Bill Gates, but well, none can question the courage he displayed.

I know, better than anyone else that even after reading the above examples, there are plenty of people out there who are skeptical about this theory of not thinking about the result. But allow me to explain in a slightly more dramatic manner.

Suppose you are in a brawl with a guy. Do you honestly think you can land the best punch if you are scared of the other guy, if you are worried about the punch the other guy is going to land, if you are really thinking about the out put of the brawl? You can land the best punch only if you are thinking about "how well you can land your punch" and of course the fight unfolds by itself.

Believe me friends . . . . Life is no different. You **just cannot** land the best punch (both literal and metaphorical) if you are worried about the punches that await you.

You may win or lose. Yes, yes, yes . . . . you may win or lose. Am sure you agree putting up a fight doesn't guarantee winning. Of course not. But, trust me friends, both in life and a fight, the biggest regrets arise because you didn't land your best punch, not because you won or lost. Some of the most painful memories arise because you have not been bold or acted courageously at the appropriate moment. Think it over my dear readers. Think in to your past. You will realize that I am not far from truth.

One of the foremost teachings of Swami Vivekananda is "Be bold & be strong. Don't worry about anything? Your Soul is strong enough to gobble up any thing that comes your way. Yah . . . Even death".

So friends . . . . you got to have the guts to become a Billionaire. No other go.

A saying I prefer to quote here before I conclude this chapter.

"A ship is never going to sink in the dock. But that's not what a ship is meant for".

So . . . . ask yourself "Am I going to be a ship that never sinks in the dock or a ship that dares into hostile territory and does what a ship is meant to do". It's for you to decide.

But remember one thing again. "A brave man dies only once. But a coward dies a thousand times."

Philanthropy; Giving Back to the World

Philanthropy conventionally means "love of humanity" in the sense of caring for, nourishing, developing and enhancing "what it is to be human" on both the benefactors (by identifying and exercising their values in giving and volunteering) and beneficiaries' (by benefitting) parts. The most conventional modern definition is "private initiatives, for public good, focusing on improving quality of others life".

Mathew 25:35

> For I was an hungred and ye gave me meat: Ye gave me meat: I was thirsty and ye gave me drink ;I was stranger, and ye took me in:

> Naked and ye clothed me; I was sick and ye visited me: I was in prison and ye came unto me

> Then shall the righteous answer him, saying, Lord, when saw we thee an hungred and fed thee? Or thirsty, and gave thee drink ?

> Or when saw we thee sick, or in prison and came unto thee?

> And the king shall answer and king shall answer
> and say unto them, verily I say unto you, In as
> much as ye have done it on to one of the least of
> these my brethren, ye have done it unto me.

What was the moral of the above teaching? Doesn't need to be a genius to know the answer. The answer is pretty evident and pretty simple.

"Be kind, help the poor and needy, heed a thought for the destitute and God is going to be pleased with you. God is going to construe your service to the poor and destitute as service to himself and you will be rewarded accordingly."

Philanthropy has become quite a common word in the super rich circles nowadays. But let me tell you philanthropy is nothing new. This concept of giving back to the society by the super rich industrialists started in early 20th century. The two fore most philanthropists of America, who were in race for riches suddenly put themselves in race for giving back to the society. Well . . . . No prizes for guessing the names!

The two gentlemen I am talking about are John Rockefeller and Andrew Carnegie. What exactly prompted them to take initiative to giveback to the society, I don't know for sure. As a matter of fact, historians have given various reasons. But one common opinion which found consensus among many a men is, both the great industrialists were sick of the adjectives "greedy and money mongers" attributed to them. They both wanted to eliminate the image that was imprinted on them by the general public. What ever the exact reason is, one credit must and must and must be given to them. They definitely initiated a trend which has gained and gaining a huge momentum in this 21st century.

A glance at the below list of 21ˢᵗ century Billionaire "givers" will give you an idea of the magnitude of momentum this idea called "giving back" has caught up in our modern society. Different billionaires have different agendas; some to uplift the education of the backward world, some to eradicate poverty, some to feed the masses, some to aid in the AIDS cure research, some to aid in the cancer cure research. But one common thing among all the contributions is that their donations are **selfless acts**. What they are doing has somewhere or other "fed the hungred, clothed the naked, took care of the sick". See the list of the Philanthropists in the table 1 who have given more than a billion dollars to the society & uplifted a billion lives.

Table 1

S.No	Name
1	Bill Gates, U.S.
2	Warren Buffett, U.S.
3	George Soros, U.S.
4	Gordon Moore, U.S.
5	Carlos Slim Helú, Mexico
6	George Kaiser, U.S.
7	Eli Broad, U.S.
8	Azim Premji, India
9	James Stowers, U.S.
10	Michael Bloomberg, U.S.
11	Li Ka-shing, Hong Kong
12	Herbert & Marion Sandler, U.S.
13	Dietmar Hopp, Germany
14	Michael Dell, U.S.

15	Jon Huntsman, U.S.
16	Ted Turner, U.S.
17	Klaus Tschira, Germany
18	Paul Allen, U.S.
19	Stephan Schmidheiny, Switzerland

As I mentioned earlier, the above gentlemen's philanthropic agendas vary from education to vaccinations to environmental protection to cancer cure research to Aids awareness. Some of the above gentlemen retired from their main stream business to dedicate themselves to Philanthropy. Some as early as 47! What joy they must be deriving out of their self less acts? And how much God must be pleased with them?

Bhagavad Gita Ch:18: Text 5

Acts of sacrifice, charity and penance are not to be given up but should be performed. Indeed; sacrifice, charity and penance purify even the great souls.

Even the pure souls are further purified! Indian sages all the way from time immemorial have always maintained that self less acts of penance and charity always elevate you to higher planets. Our Indian sages' stance is . . . you help lower human beings (mind you . . . . am not degrading anyone when I say lower human beings . . . I only mean lesser previleged) and you will be helped by more evolved beings closer to the supreme. Whether the more evolved beings are in this world or in higher worlds! My personal belief is that blessings and good wishes come true. They indeed materialize. They some how or other aid in giving something good back to you. And I personally strongly believe and as a matter of fact know personally that good and bad we give come back in equal measure.

Read the three verses from Bhagavad Gita mentioned below.

Bhagavad Gita Ch:16 verse 1-3

The blessed lord said: fearlessness, purification of one's existence, enhancement of the spiritual knowledge, charity, self-control, performance of sacrifice, studying Vedas, austerity and simplicity; non violence, truth-fullness, freedom from anger, renunciation, tranquility, aversion to fault finding, compassion and freedom from cunningness, gentleness, modesty and steady determination; vigor, forgiveness, fortitude, cleanliness, freedom from envy and the passion for honor—these transcendental qualities son of Bharata, belong to godly men endowed with divine nature.

Bhagavad Gita Ch:17 verse 25

One should perform sacrifice, penance and charity with the word tat. The purpose of such transcendental activities is to get free from the material engagement

Bhagavad Gita Ch:18 Verse 26-27

The absolute truth is the objective of devotional sacrifice, and it is indicated by word sat. These works of sacrifice, of penance and of charity, true to the absolute nature, are performed to please the supreme, O son of Partha.

Getting a hang of the importance of charity? Seeing the glimpse of the emphasis of charity? Lord Krishna or Jesus Christ wouldn't have mentioned umpteen number of times the importance of charity In their tutelage just like that. Would they? Are you able to relate how impeccably the billionaires are practicing one of the very important parts of the preachings? I hope my dear readers see the point.

Bhagavad Gita Ch:18 Verse 6

All these activities should be performed without any expectation of result. They should be performed as a matter of duty, O son of Partha. That is my final opinion.

Read the above verse again and again and again. Do these *activities without any expectation of result.* Doing something good for others without expectation of any result may call for highest level of kindness or rather godliness. As a matter of fact, it may even appear to be too idealistic. But that's the point. Some of the greatest billionaires have performed some extreme selfless acts. Martin Luther King Jr, Mother Teresa, Mahatma Gandhi, Abraham Lincoln . . . . did any of the above ladies & gentlemen have anything to profit at a personal level from their acts? Their entire efforts were directed in uplifting the masses, millions of them. And today billions are enjoying the benefits of their acts of benevolence and sacrifice.

I would like to inform you that my journey of philanthropy started when I was an ordinary salaried guy (Even now, am a salaried guy ☺). I'll inform you, what is the actual verse which propelled me into giving something back to the society.

Proverbs 3:9 &3:10

Honour the lord with thy Substance, and with
the first fruits of all thine increase:

So shall thy barns be filled with plenty, and thy
presses shall burst out with thy wine.

I started donating a fixed fraction of my salary to two
charitable organizations regularly and I firmly believe that
my act of goodness has stood by me in good stead. Ok, I
admit that my donations are not anywhere on par with the
huge amounts some of the above billionaires have donated.
But in my limits, I did something good and I am proud of
it. And let me tell you that one of the two organizations I
donated to is a Christian organization and another, a Hindu
temple.

I must admit I was selfish when I started donating. I
must admit every time I gave something to some charitable
organization, I expected something in return. I was as a
matter of fact demanding during my daily prayers saying "I
am giving something to the society, so I want that in return,
I want this in return". It was only a matter of time I realized
how foolish I have been. I decided to leave the returns to
the creator. As a matter of fact, I decide to even to leave the
decision to whether to return anything to me or not to the
god lord himself. And just like that one fine day, this idea to
write this book just came into my mind. Woosh !! And it just
flashed into my mind and it stayed there. I construe this idea
given to me as a reward for my acts of Charity. I honestly
don't know what destiny has in store for me. But I made a
commitment to myself that irrespective of my income, I
am going to give regularly a fraction of my monthly salary
to some charitable organization which strives for some good

cause. And I whole heartedly appeal to you through this book, my dear readers. Give something, anything . . . . how ever minuscule it may appear. And take my word friends. You will be rewarded one way or another.

More and more super successful personalities are surely but steadily realizing that giving back to the society is as important as getting something out of society. More and more are realizing that spending a part of their colossal fortune for helping the poor and homeless needy better be a commitment than an obligation. From Bill Gates to Oprah Winfrey to Halle Berry to Azim Premji to Nandan Nilekani (Co founder of Infosys), more and more billionaires are committing themselves to donate larger and larger fraction of their income to the upbringing of the poor in one way or another. Many billionaires are establishing their own foundations or charity organizations. Some billionaires have donated fraction of their incomes to other charitable organizations. Warren buffet has donated till date more than a billion dollars to the Bill and Melinda Gates Foundation founded ofcourse by Bill Gates.

Of course, like every good act, even philanthropy is being met by some or other criticism. Some say Billionaires donate sizeable amounts for saving on tax, some say they do for getting good name, some say that they donate as a pre-requisite for entering politics; some say it's an image building for better public relations. But to hell with what some road going ***ordinary*** people say. They are indeed ordinary people. Why pay heed to them? Why bother about them?

Follow your heart. Do it because two of the greatest representatives of god have recommended (mind you, I use the word recommend, not ordered or commanded) you to do so. A small thought or a very personal interpretation that flashed into my mind is, God could have instilled philanthropy or desire to give back as something natural to human beings like thirst or hunger. But he didn't. One small sensitive desire of the creator would have been, human beings must do something good to fellow human beings by their own self. Human beings should feel the pinch in their hearts to give some thing back as a self motivated urge, not because they are compelled.

So my dear readers do something good. For god's sake . . . . For good's sake. Do it. That's what many of the Billionaires are doing. Well, try to imitate at least. Who knows this may be the act which may be your first step in becoming billionaire. Who knows?

Swami Vivekananda says "Don't stand on a high pedestal and give a beggar a cent and feel proud of yourself. As a matter of fact, it's because of the beggar that you are having the privilege of doing something good."

So avail yourself of your privilege. You have already been given it.

Swami Parmahansa Yogananda preaches "God checks how much one feels for their fellowmen and his own children"

Malachi 3:10

Bring all the tithes into the storehouse, that there may be meat in mine house, and prove me now herewith, saith the lord of hosts, if I will not open you the windows of heaven, and pour you out a blessing, that there shall not be room enough to receive it.

Well, my dear readers, does the above verse re-iterate the fact that you are going to be richly rewarded if you do one thing . . . . "Give".

Give something back to the society; what ever your pocket permits.It is worth giving a try, my dear readers. One thing I assure you, you are going to feel a lot better about yourself. If you, as a true Christian or a Hindu, believe in every alphabet of the scripture, am sure you won't have any problem implementing what has been preached in this chapter. And start doing because, nowadays every billionaire is doing so.

Hence, try "Giving".

MY PERSONAL OPINION AND THE SUMMARY

As I went about speaking about the various traits that are embedded in a super successful human being and the similarities between the billionaires and the preachings, I must admit, I myself have a long way to go before I call myself a billionaire in any field. I myself am yet to implement a lot of things I mentioned in the previous chapters. I myself am yet to absorb into my veins and blood the teachings of the two celestials masters. But writing this book has definitely been a start for me and completing this book has definitely given me confidence that there is something in me that makes me stand out of the crowd . . . . After all, what percentage of human beings on this planet have authored a book successfully? One in hundred? One in two hundred? . . . . I don't know the exact stats . . . . but my chest certainly swells with pride when I look myself in the mirror.

One question has always intrigued me ever since I attained a certain level of adulthood and once I realized the mortality of my own self. "Am I going to be one among the several ants that live and die on this earth . . . . only difference . . . . ant lives for 7 days and I live for 70 years? Am I going to be one among the *ordinary* billions of people who grow up to find a secure job, raise their family with 2 kids, retire and go to grave?" . . . . NO . . . . NO . . . .

NO . . . . I refused to be and writing this book is definitely a start for that refusal.

I always believed (strictly my belief . . . . you are most welcome to disagree) in the philosophy that after life we all will have to answer God. God is definitely going to ask "I have given you 60-70 years of time on earth . . . . what on earth have you been doing?". God definitely knows the answer, but nevertheless he asks and I want to give a profound substantial answer to the almighty. Writing this book is my first step in preparing for that answer on the judgment day. Surely completion of this book is going to add to my resume called "Life". Am pretty sure and none can argue with the fact that all the billionaires have some superlative answers ready.

And I *also* firmly believe in what Swami Vivekananda said over a century ago in one of his famous lectures in London.

"All the powers are already ours. Infinite strength, Infinite freedom, Infinite power is already ours. All the gods, deities, goddesses are right there inside us. It is we who put palms across our eyes and think there is darkness in front of us. It is we who enchain our self to mental chains and think ourself bonded. Nothing is impossible to our soul, considering ourselves weak is the only sin we can ever do."

Author of one of the most acclaimed self improvement books "Awaken the Giant Within", Anthony Robbins further corroborated the above fact. All the enthusiasm, all the will power, all the necessary resources any human being needs to achieve anything is within our body and the mind present within. All we need to do is to believe in that fact and be willing to access the resources present within in a conscious manner. I believe I did.

Of course, I have certainly not done anything impossible. I certainly am not any extra-ordinary human being . . . . writing a book is nothing new after all . . . . but it is nothing common either. But today, I know that there is a spark in me and spark can be turned into fire with right magnitude of fuel (hard work).After all, any ultra efficient gasoline engine which powers any Ferrari is nothing but a machine which is capable of producing spark after spark after spark. The higher the frequency with which the machine is capable of producing the spark, better the pickup of the vehicle and better the performance of the vehicle.

Well . . . . if any one of the readers thinks I am bragging, you bet I am. Yah, I am bragging the hell out of myself. But none who so ever it is can refute what I said in the previous paragraph. As the one and the only Muhammad Ali said "you are not bragging if you can back it (what you said) up with deeds".

One more strong belief I have is, the very fact you are reading this book means that you are blessed, guided and protected. Who can disprove that providence himself directed this book into your hands. I personally believe two of the greatest Avatars and representatives of god who ever walked on this earth in flesh and blood, Lord Krishna and Lord Jesus Christ cast a merciful (a.k.a loving) eye on me and picked me up for writing this book. When I got the idea to write this book, I took it as an honor and privilege. I am proclaiming to the world that Billionaires are not miles away from religion, but as a matter of fact, there is a higher level of religion in the billionaires than in among common men.

And who knows? Perhaps, the same two Avatars have guided you to pick up this book. Well, this, you can interpret the way you want and I'll leave it you. Nevertheless, I request you in the feeblest voice possible. Imagine, at least try to imagine, that these two gods have directed your footsteps to this book. Do you feel any boost in your self esteem? Do you feel your pride hiked up by the very thought itself? I hope so. If the above imagination is your belief or even conviction, there can be nothing better than that.

I am 100% sure that you are definitely spiritually inclined if you have picked up this book. And I am more than 100 % sure of another fact about you, my dear reader. You have been hit real badly at some juncture of your life (just like me), one way or other and that pain has steered you to the spiritual path (just like me). And am equally sure, it is the same path that has driven you towards this book (consciously or subconsciously). And it is totally up to you what you choose.

Whether to put into daily use what you have learnt or realized after you read this book or to ignore if you do

not find my opinions to your approval . . . . It's totally up to you. After all, I am also a human being and how much ever study I made before writing this book, I am sure my personal opinions and takeaways must have been sprinkled here and there.

As I mentioned in one of the previous chapters, what happens to you doesn't matter. It's what you decide to do with the happening which matters.

Well, this book "happened" to you. So what are you going to do about it? It is your choice. But please remember . . . .

Proverbs 13:8

Poverty and Shame shall be to them that refuseth instruction.

Nope, neither am I threatening you nor am I putting a gun to your head to follow every letter I said in the book. As a matter of fact, I have not preached anything. All I did was to bring to your notice what has been preached by the great masters in the light of contemporary times. I am only appealing to you to try to implement the instructions given in the two great books and save your self from poverty or mediocrity in life, when God himself has so clearly encouraged you to seek the kingdom *you so richly deserve*.

A brief introduction to everyone about my own spiritual journey! When I started reading Bible and Bhagavad Gita, I was at the lowest point of my life. As a matter of fact, I thought these religious books are meant for grim faced losers who have accepted defeat with their lives. But as I read on, I understood some truths. Yes, they are truths, not my opinions nor my interpretations nor my beliefs. They are absolute truths. As irrefutable as "Sun rises from the east"! The truths are . . . .

Every man is a born winner.

The very fact that we are selected to be human beings makes us a winner.

We already are high manifestations of god.

Bhagavad Gita Chapter 7, Text 5

Besides this inferior nature, O mighty armed Arjuna, there is a superior Energy of mine, which are all living entities who are all struggling with material nature and are sustaining the universe.

Yes, you are all the manifestations of superior energy of god

We are unique creations of the creator.

We already belong to the "top brass", "high command" of the world.

We are already very special in the God's scheme of this world.

The Superlative greats have only manifested the godliness in them at a higher level.

I reiterate, there is a divine spark in each and every one of us. Yes it is there in YOU. Yes, yes, yes . . . . my dear reader. I am talking to YOU. And it is an eternal truth.

More importantly, I clearly realize one more thing in the hind sight. The deep hurt which brought me to my lowest point was merely a pointer towards the priceless, timeless (and always timely) wisdom preached in those 2 great books. God wanted me to read these two great books and several great books & classics I read hence forth.God wanted to impart some of the highest wisdom to me. He loves me (and of course everybody in this world) after all. That's exactly why he hurt me like hell. Oh yeah . . . . God knows how to show you hell on earth ☺. (Perhaps, you can tweak this above paragraph as per your convenience. Am sure you can relate it to your life).But like any grown up wise adult, I am steadily but surely realizing one fact of life.

Everything indeed happens for a reason.

Allow me to explain in a slightly dramatic & cinematic manner.

Almost everyone must have seen the Classic Kungfu Cult movie "Enter the Dragon" several times. Please recollect the scene of Bruce lee's tutelage to the young student in the very early part of the movie.

The conversation goes like this.

Bruce lee gives a kick to the young boy and asks "How did that feel to you?"

Boy: "Let me think"

Bam!! A slap on the boy's forehead.

Bruce lee: "Don't think . . . . Feeeeeeeeeeeel!! It is like a finger pointing away to the moon."

Another Bam!!! Lee catches the boy looking at the finger.

Bruce lee: **Don't** concentrate on the finger or you will miss **all** the heavenly glory

Read the last sentence once again.

"Don't concentrate on the finger or you will miss all the heavenly glory"

Perhaps or shall I say, most probably, the pain or hurt which you are brooding about *is nothing but* a finger pointing away to some invaluable lesson or priceless wisdom or some divine purpose for which you have been brought onto this earth a.k.a heavenly glory. Almost everybody is concentrating on the hurt (finger).

How could he do this to me?

Why did this happen to me?

Does god have anything against me?

Why am I such a loser?

What have I done to deserve this?

Blah . . . blah . . . . blah . . . .

All the above questions do nothing but lead us to self pity, frustration, anger. All, anyone in the right mind should do is to raise their eyes and look at the Wisdom (The heavenly glory), the hurt (finger) is pointing at.

Arnold Schwarzenegger at the end of his Auto Biography "Total Recall; My unbelievably True Story" recalls how the traumatizing childhood (finger) he underwent thanks to the strict disciplinarian father drove him towards the liberal lands of United States of America (heavenly glory).I have seen a forty year old man who blamed his drunkard father, who passed away fourteen years before (at the time of my talk with him) for his today's financial mess. What a shame!! If only that gentleman can take a page out of Arnold's life. If only anyone, who blames their childhood or unhappy home for their current state can take a page out of Arnold's life!

George Bush.Sr recites how his coming face to face with the carnage of war, almost getting killed in one of his bombing missions at a very young age (finger) shaped his conviction by which he stood by all his life. The conviction was "stand up to the evil come what may (Heavenly glory)". It was the same conviction which made him send the armed forces into Kuwait to counter the aggression of Saddam Husain, the Iraqi dictator. And world knows what a huge crisis was averted. Just imagine, how the world would have looked if Saddam had control over all the oil resources in the Middle East.

Viktor Frankl, amidst the inhuman atrocities (finger) in the Nazi holocaust realized that there is one last frontier of freedom which no one can breach into . . . . the human mind (Heavenly glory). His refusal to let his inner world to be affected by the outer world, how ever repugnant it was lead the whole world to believe that a human is indeed capable of choosing any reaction he wants. No wonder, the gentleman's name surfaces in almost every Self Improvement book I came across.

I can give you umpteen numbers of similar examples where and when some extreme adverse conditions (the finger) brought out the true mettle and steel(heavenly glory) out of the great men and women. I clearly understand that it's that realization of their own true potential & mettle which served as a fulcrum for facing and surviving all the battles that they waged and won for rest of their lives. As a matter of fact, the more adverse the conditions they faced and won over in early phases of their lives, the greater they become. Their adverse conditions and traumatizing situations were the very "Defining moments" which shaped their destiny. The billionaires used these defining moments as a spring board to jump up high in their lives. Yes, they consciously decided to jump **up** in their life. It is in these defining moments they got the "call from their higher self". They answered, they obeyed, and they backed themselves. And I need not re-iterate how their lives have served the world as beacons of light, inspiration, hope & courage to Billions of people.

Dear Readers, I hope you see that I am completing the loop here.I am back to the first chapter. As I mentioned in the first chapter, your call from higher self is around the corner of a deep pain.

The Entire Summary of Bhagavad Gita is

"*What ever happened has happened for good, what ever is happening is happening for good, What ever is going to happen is also for good". A small addition from my side. All we have to do is to look for something good in every thing*". Did any one say positive thinking is a new concept? No offense Dr.Peale (Author of Power of Positive thinking, a must read book for any one who wants to grow up in life).

As I went about looking for something good during my lowest point of my life, I recognized the heavenly glory that was shown to me and realized (Okay . . . . not 100 % yet . . . . I myself have a long way to go) the above mentioned truths.

And the above truths can be realized (please understand the difference between intellectually knowing and realizing) by everybody if they apply themselves. There is certainly a spark in every one & with the right fuel, anyone can turn the sparks inside them into fires. This truth is already a fully realized truth for any billionaire, any superlative successful human being and any "the best" in his or her field.

They answered the call from their higher soul(Ch.1), they believed that they are capable(Ch.2), they worked their butts out to achieve the goal(Ch.3), they refused to be ruffled by the ups and downs or give into fears that come their way(Ch.4), they confronted their adversities head on(Ch.5) and they did win finally. After they won, they realised the importance of giving back to the society and they did (Ch.6).

There is common flaw in people's way of thinking . . . . that all billionaires are some kind of prodigies towards whom God has been partial and who are divinely gifted with some rare talent from birth. Indeed there is some truth in the above. Some people (Bill Gates for eg.) exhibit precocious talent in some fields right from the word go. But to be successful, being a child prodigy is not an absolute pre-requisite. Nope, not at all.

Click on the below links (or type the below links into your internet browser), read all the below stories and you will see that not all the superlatively rich had a fairytale starts, but were ordinary people who through sheer grit and determination made their lives into fairy tales. As a matter of fact, some of them had sub standard starts. Some of them impoverished. Some of them are illiterate. One of them an illiterate woman with an alcoholic husband! Type the below links into your browser and see for yourself.

http://business.rediff.com/slide-show/2010/sep/15/slide-show-1-success-story-of-dosa-plaza.htm

http://business.rediff.com/slide-show/2010/sep/14/slide-show-1-interview-with-dilip-kapur-founder-of-hidesign.htm

http://business.rediff.com/slide-show/2010/aug/13/slide-show-1-candle-seller-to-multi-millionaire.htm#contentTop

http://business.rediff.com/slide-show/2010/jun/08/slide-show-1-from-50-paise-to-rs-2-lakh-a-day-success-story.htm

http://www.toptenz.net/top-10-rags-to-riches-stories.php

http://www.smartmoneydaily.com/celeb-finance/10-rags-to-riches-billionaires.aspx

http://www.huffingtonpost.com/2010/08/17/rags-to-riches-worlds-ric_n_671253.html

I really insist, read the above stories from internet

Am sure you can find a lot of rags to riches stories in internet and you will find out reading such stories can be more inspiring than reading about Bill Gates or Larry Ellison or Akio Morito (Founder of SONY). If an illiterate woman selling tea on a beach can make it big why can't I? If any ordinary graduate from not so impressive background can make it big in the field of consulting, why can't I? As a matter of fact if anyone can make it big . . . . Why can't I? Why can't you? Yes, Yes, Yes . . . . Why can't YOU? Yah . . . . Am challenging you.

Ask yourself the same question. Challenge yourself, Provoke yourself and prove yourself to yourself and rest of the world acknowledging your billionaire status will follow automatically.

I would conclude this book with the following suggestions and commands from Lord Jesus Christ and Lord Krishna.

Mathew 5:14
Ye are the light of the world

Mathew 5:16
Let your light so shine before men, that they may see your good works and glorify your father which is in heaven

Bhagavad-Gita:Chapter11: verse 12
If hundreds of thousands of suns rose up at once into the sky, they might resemble the effulgence of supreme person in that universal form.

I sincere hope you are that person whose light shines so bright that your effulgence eclipses the brightness of thousand suns.

I would consider this effort of mine a success, even if one person in this world says that this book has served as an eye opener or fulcrum or starting point for his superlative success journey. 25 years down the line, if any billionaire declares that this book was a kick-start for his superlative success, I would consider this effort of mine vindicated.

All the best my dear friends. I mean it. Oh yeah . . . . I really do.

Love & regards,
Vamsi Palem.

AFTER NOTE

As I went on to shower lavish praise on several super successful people and billionaires, I know better than anyone that my poor words definitely don't do justice to the greatness of the great men and women I mentioned. The 2-3 paragraphs I wrote about them only show the tip of the iceberg to say the least. I very very strongly recommend you to go through the lives of all the great people. Buy their autobiographies whenever possible and read through the lives. Trust me, there is a profound lesson in each and every chapter of their autobiographies. Any lesson you learn and implement from them can be life turning or life changing. The monetary investment on such books is definitely worth it.

Having come this far with me, I hope you agree unconditionally with out a second thought. "Leaders are Readers". All the leaders, political or spiritual or business are by default voracious readers. So why not read the lives of super greats? And see for your self how there is a lot of Bible and Bhagavad-Gita in them. You will be surprised ☺ . . . . just like me.